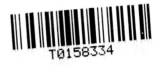

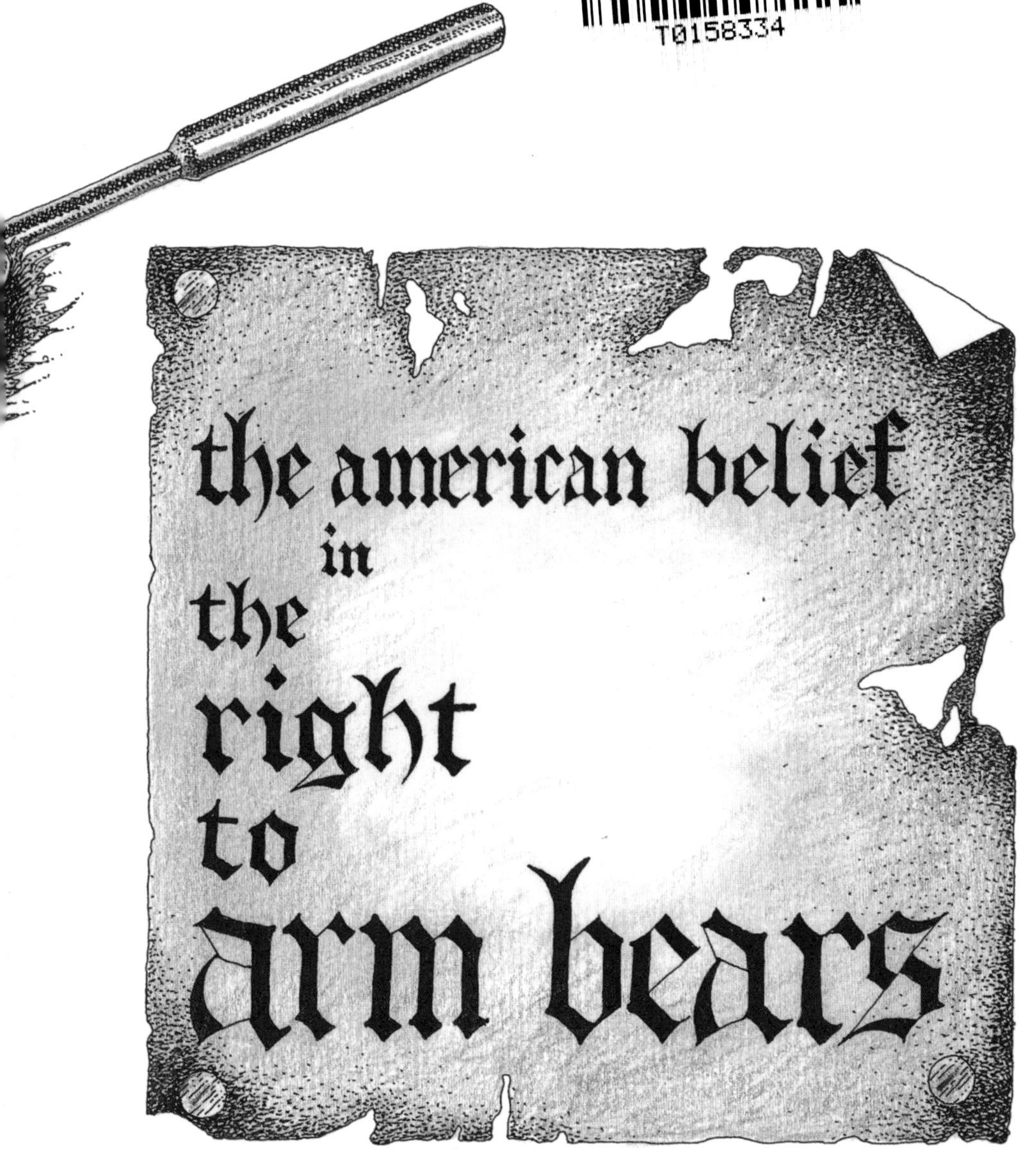
the american belief
in
the
right
to
arm bears

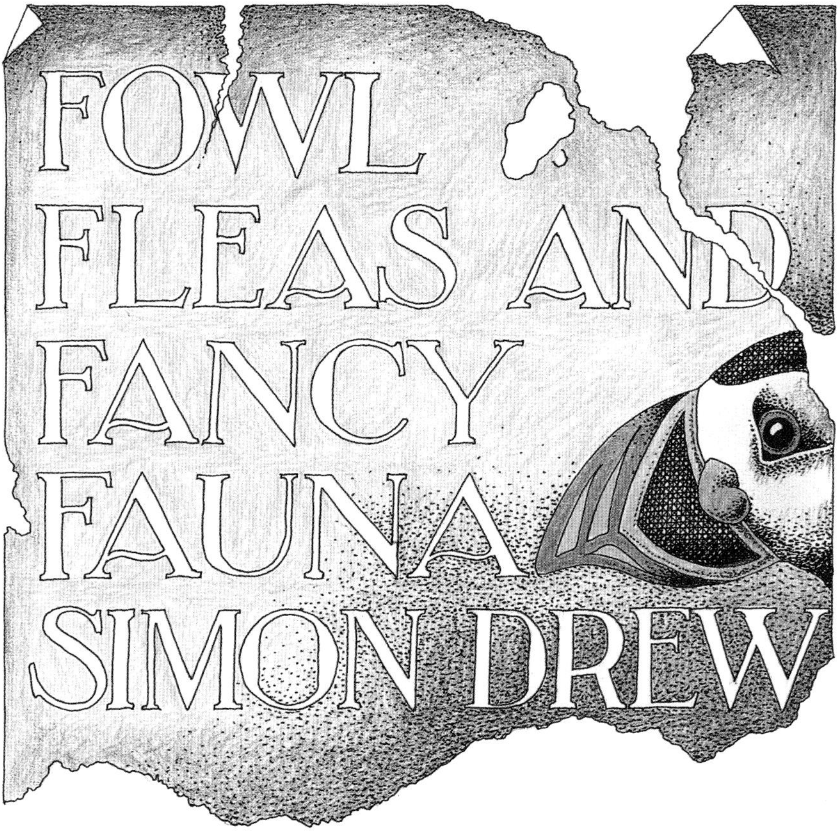
FOWL
FLEAS AND
FANCY
FAUNA
SIMON DREW

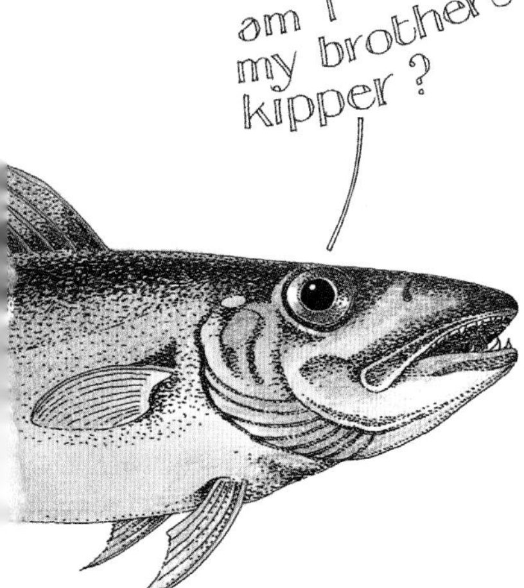
am I
my brother's
kipper ?

ACC ART BOOKS

to caroline

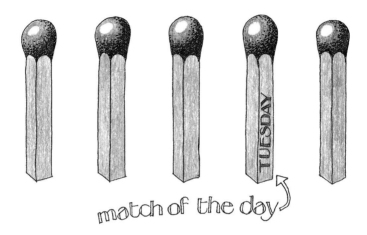

match of the day

©2015 Simon Drew
World copyright reserved

ISBN 978-1-85149-812-3

British Library Cataloguing-in-Publication Data
A catalogue record for this book is available from the British Library

All rights reserved. No part of this publication may be reproduced, stored in a
retrieval system, or transmitted in any form or by any means electronic, mechanical,
photocopying, recording or otherwise, without the prior permission of the publisher

The right of Simon Drew to be identified as author of this work has been asserted by
him in accordance with the Copyright, Designs and Patents Act 1988

FSC
www.fsc.org
MIX
Paper from
responsible sources
FSC® C104723

Printed in China
for ACC Art Books Ltd., Woodbridge, Suffolk, U.K.

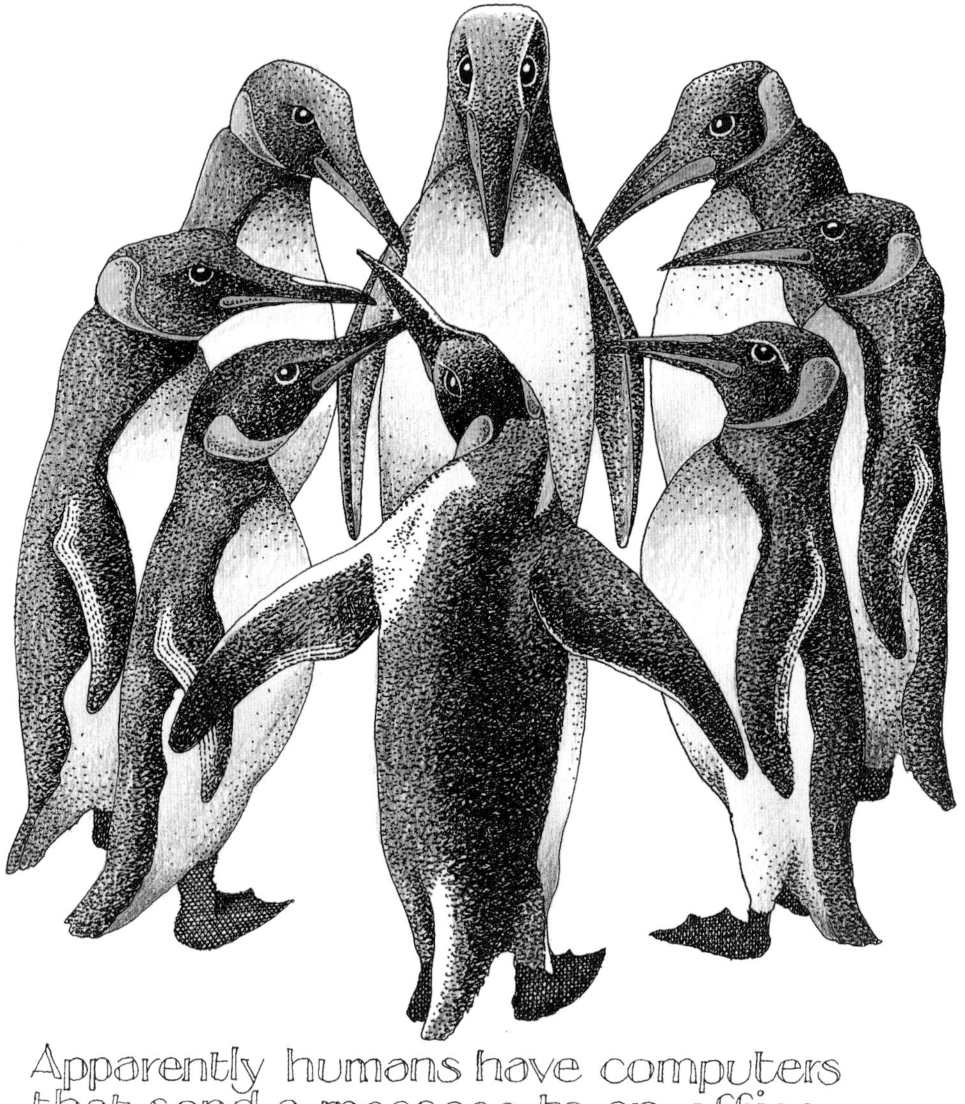

Apparently humans have computers
that send a message to an office
that sends a message to a warehouse
that sends a message to a van
that will deliver them a fish.

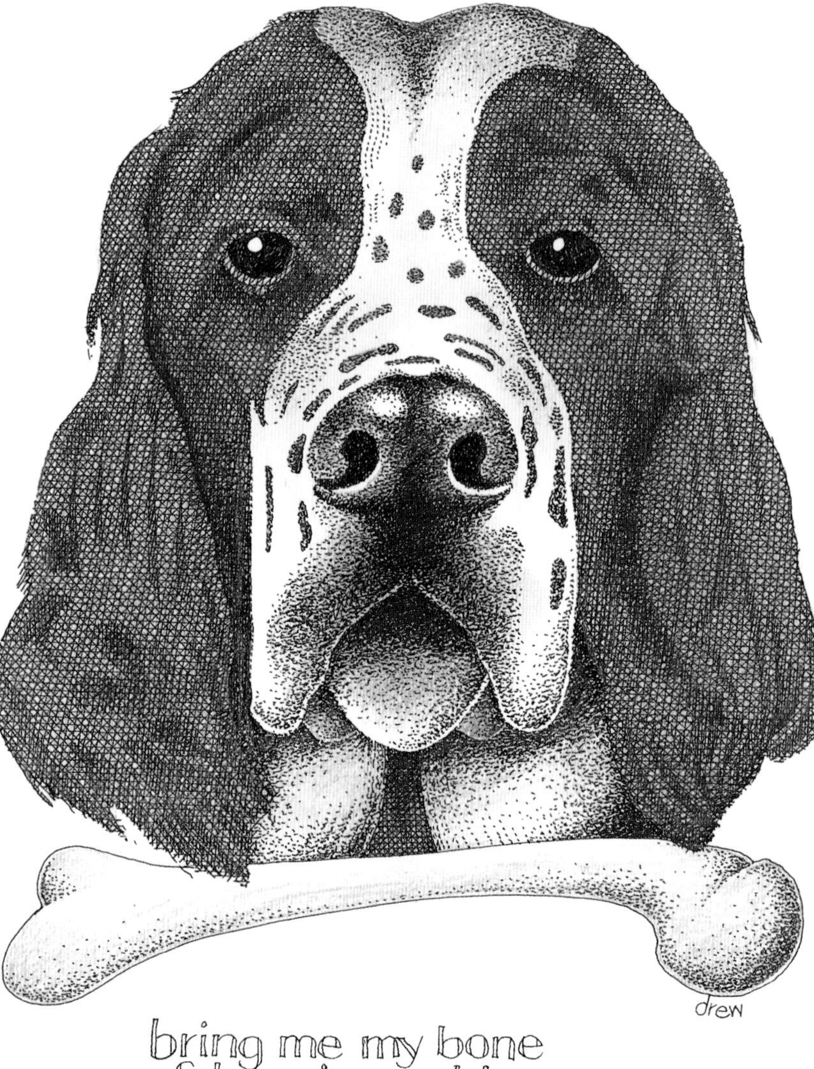
drew

bring me my bone
of burning gold
bring me my marrows
of desire.

SPOT THE SHAKESPEARE PLAY

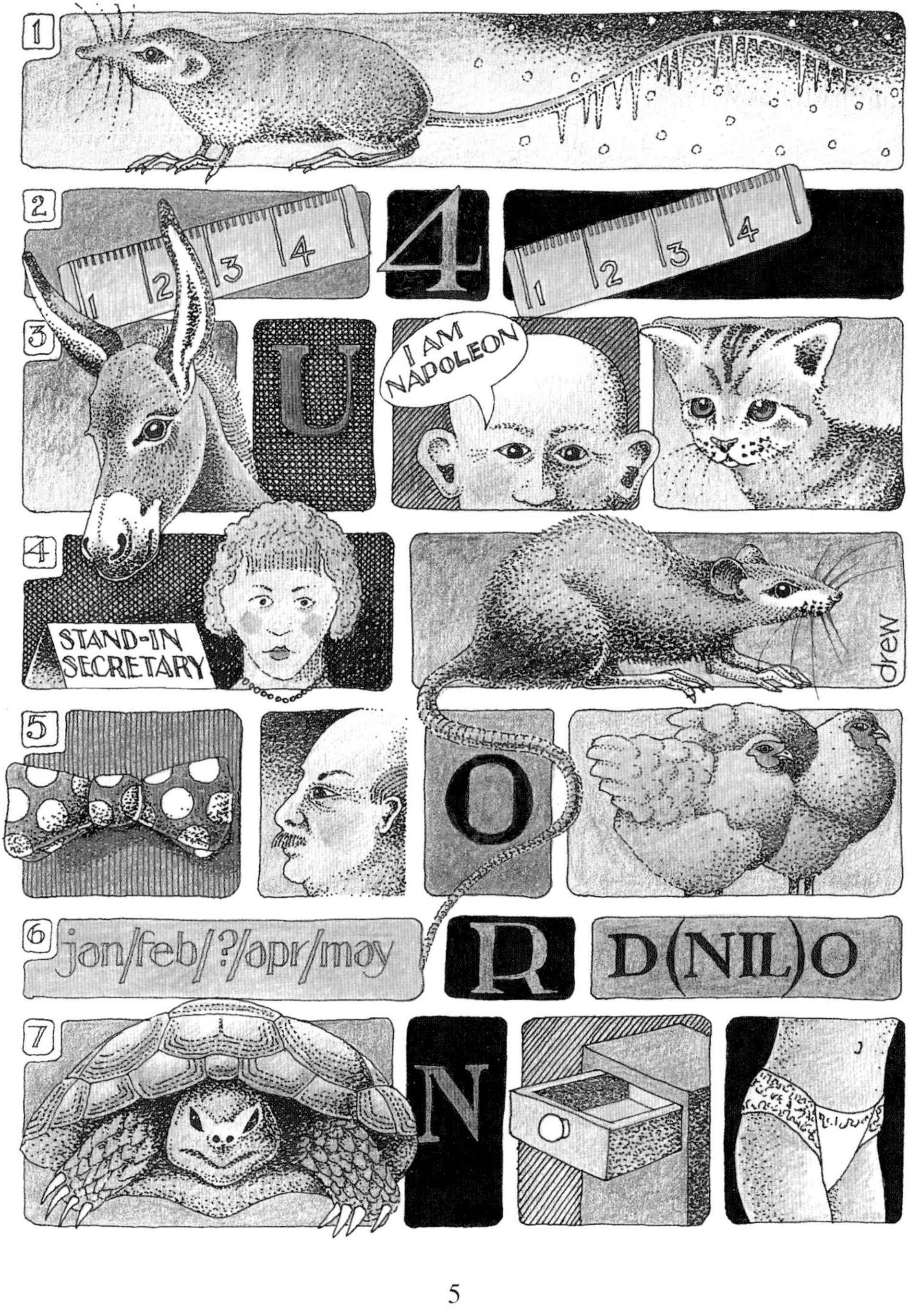
1
2
4
3
I AM NAPOLEON
U
4
STAND-IN SECRETARY
drew
5
O
6
jan/feb/?/apr/may
R
D(NIL)O
7
N

HOW TO RECOGNISE A SAILOR:

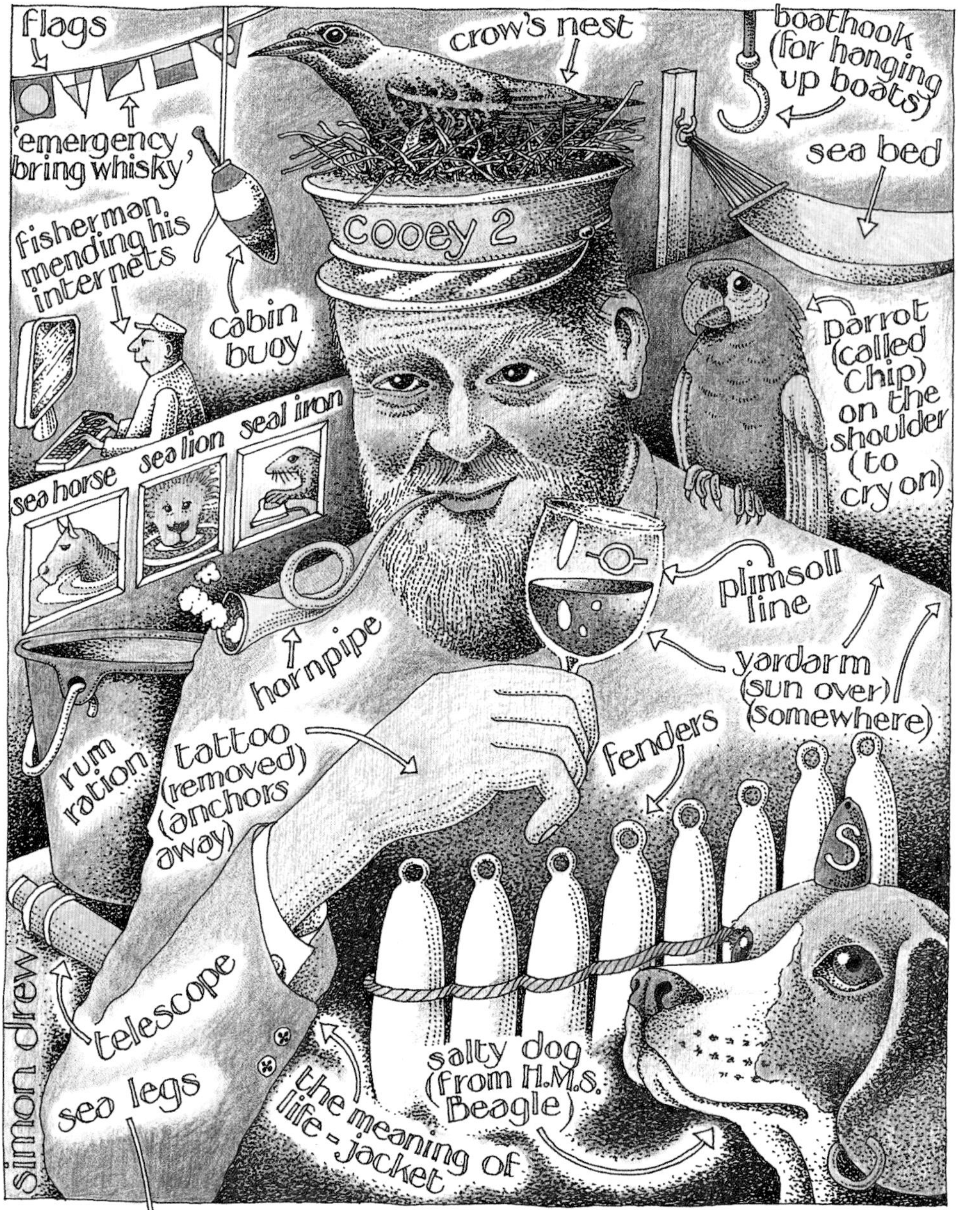

flags
'emergency bring whisky'
crow's nest
boathook (for hanging up boats)
sea bed
fisherman mending his internets
cabin buoy
COOEY 2
parrot (called Chip) on the shoulder (to cry on)
sea horse
sea lion
seal iron
plimsoll line
hornpipe
yardarm (sun over) (somewhere)
rum ration
tattoo (removed) (anchors away)
fenders
S
telescope
sea legs
the meaning of life-jacket
salty dog (from H.M.S. Beagle)
simon drew

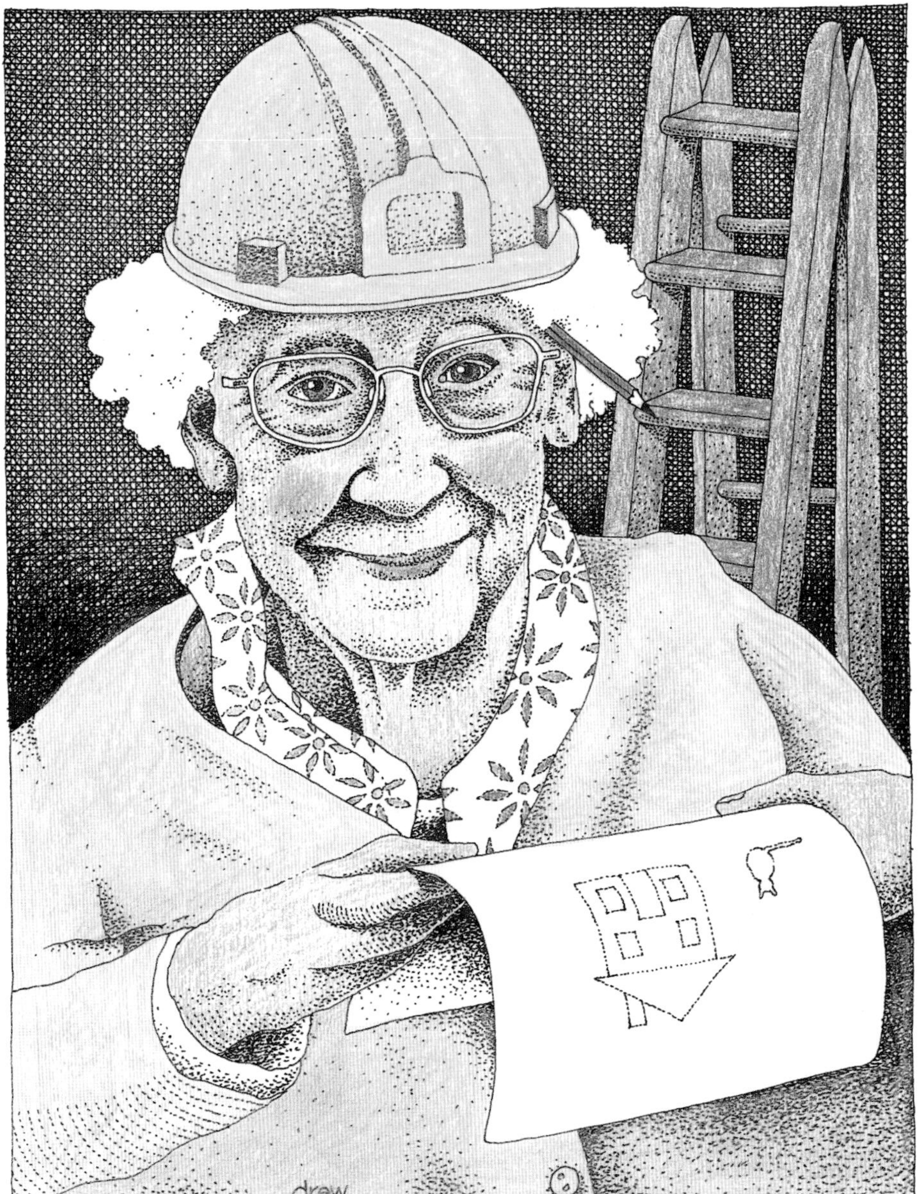
drew

GRAN DESIGNS

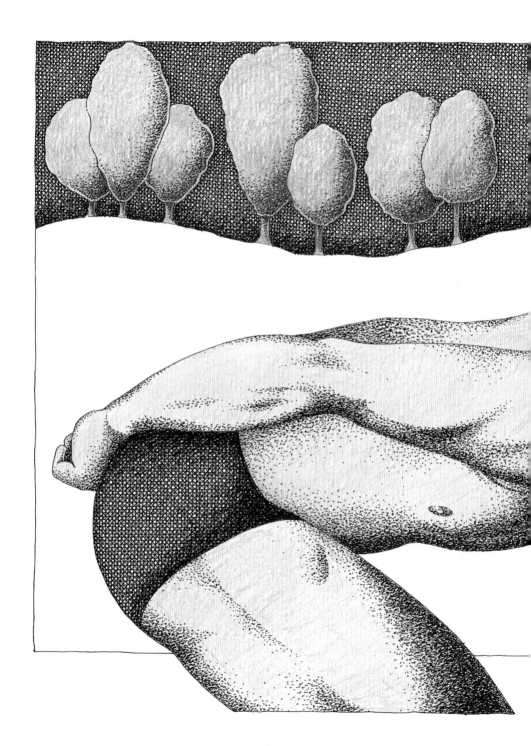

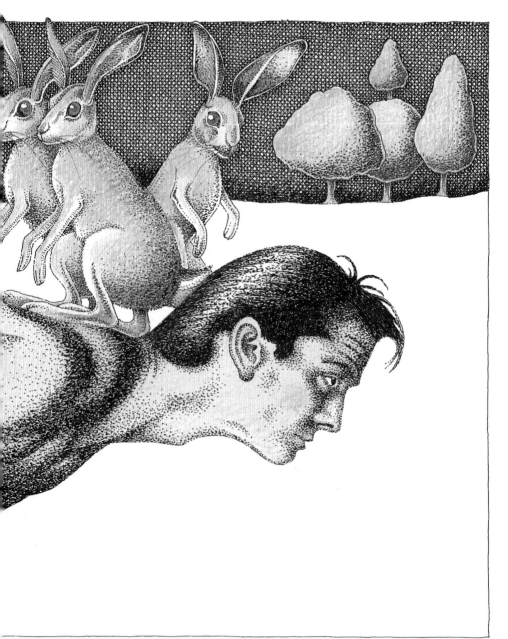

suddenly the hares on the back
of my neck stood up

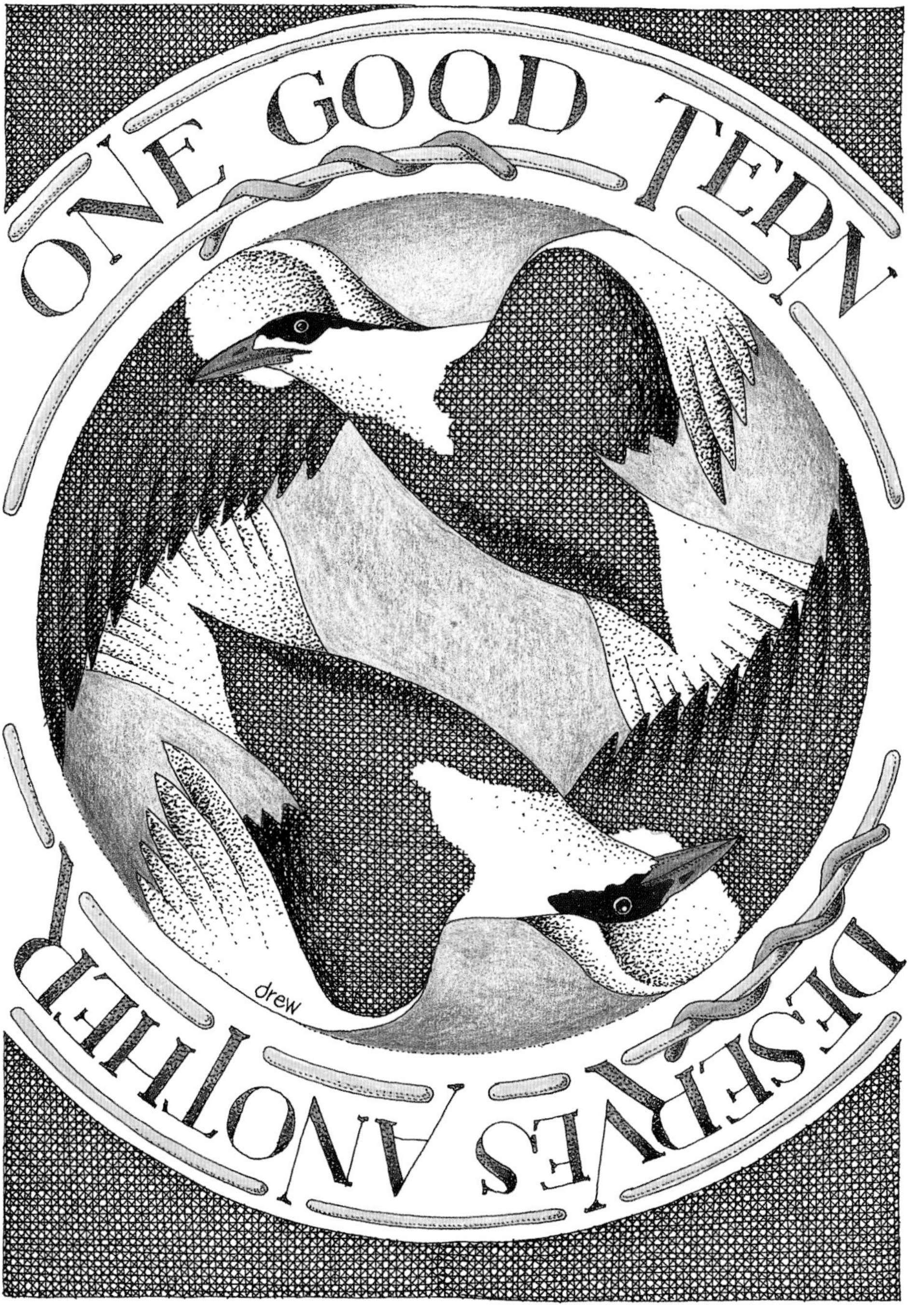
ONE GOOD TERN
DESERVES ANOTHER
drew

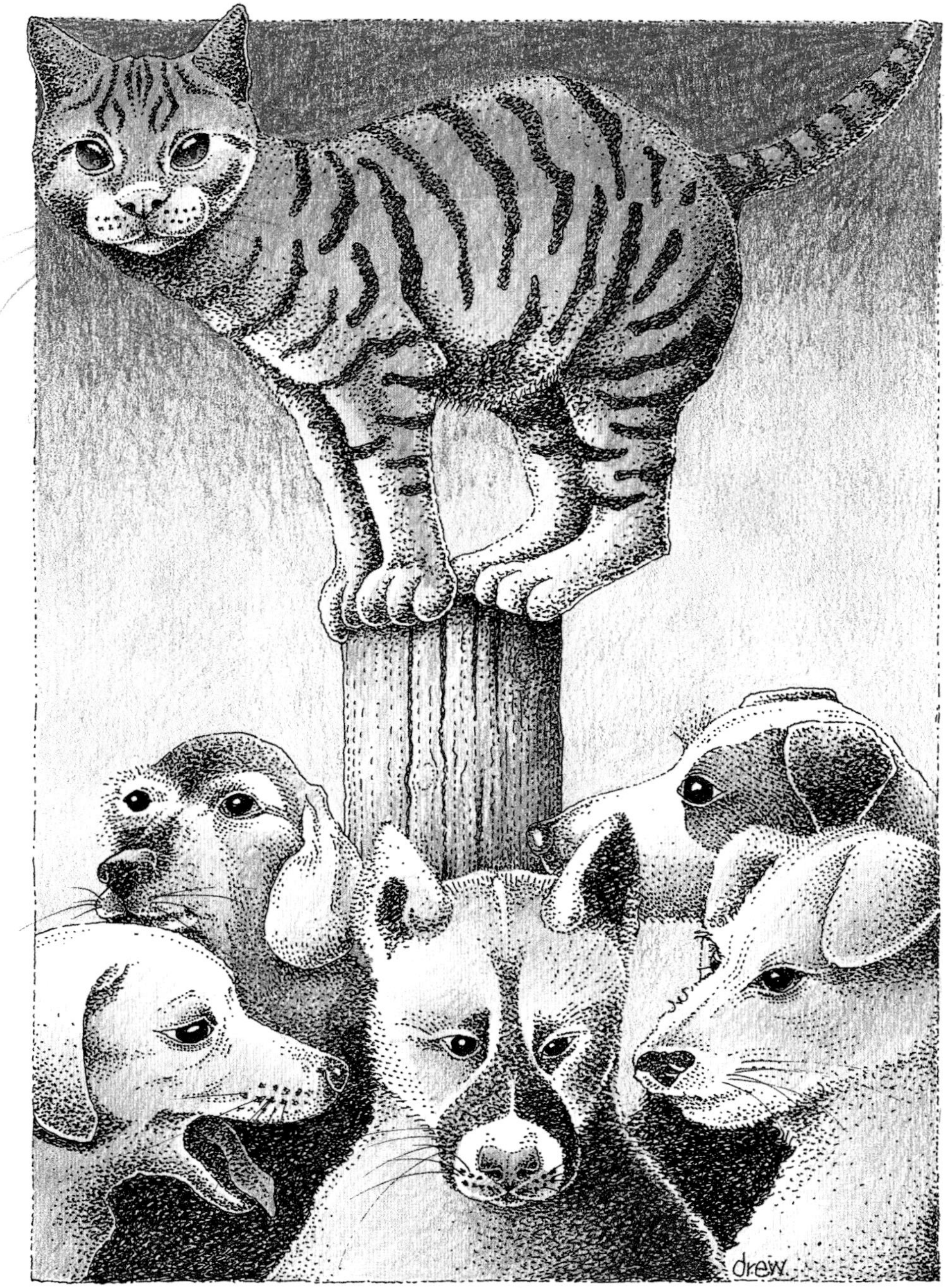
drew.

a cat above the rest

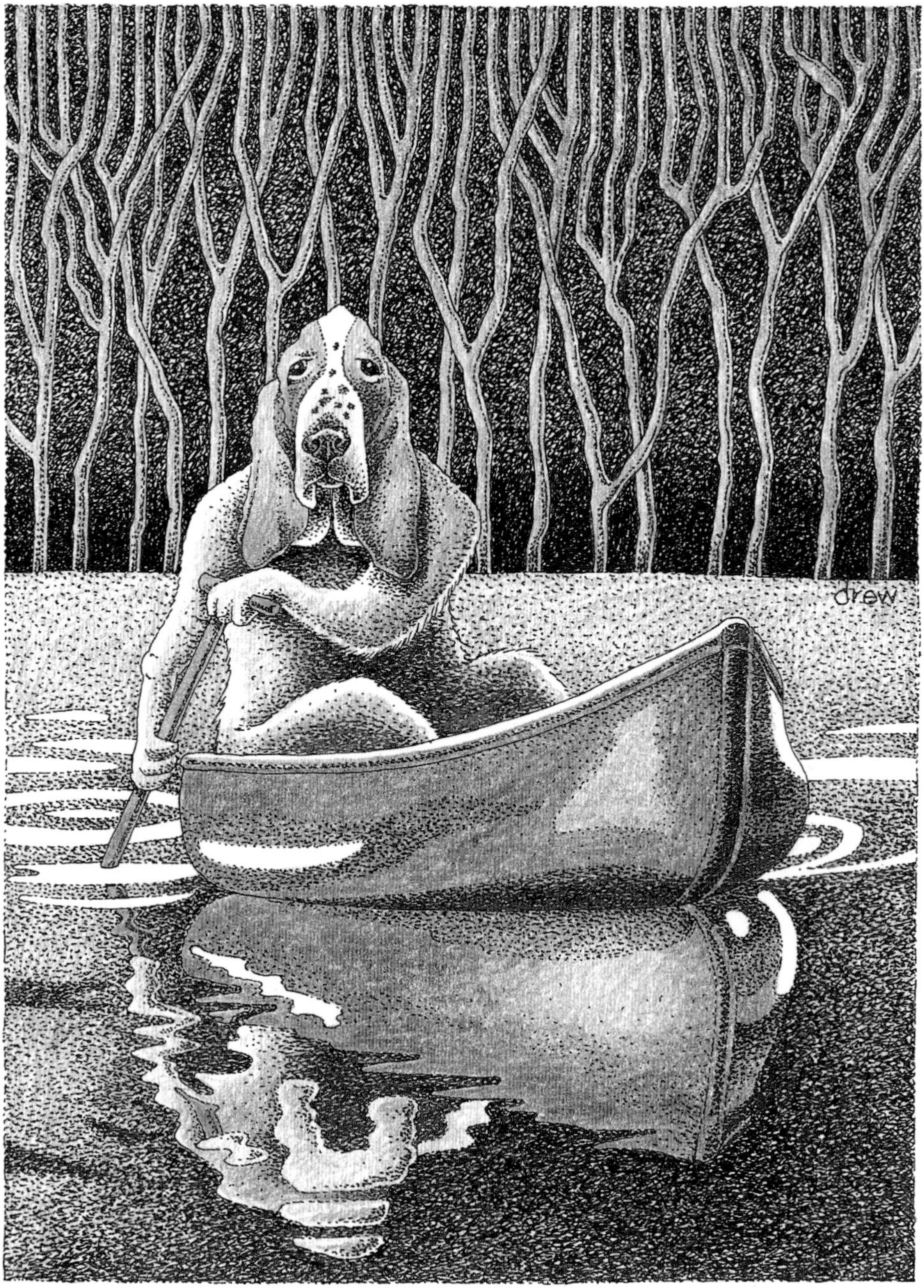
drew

doggypaddle

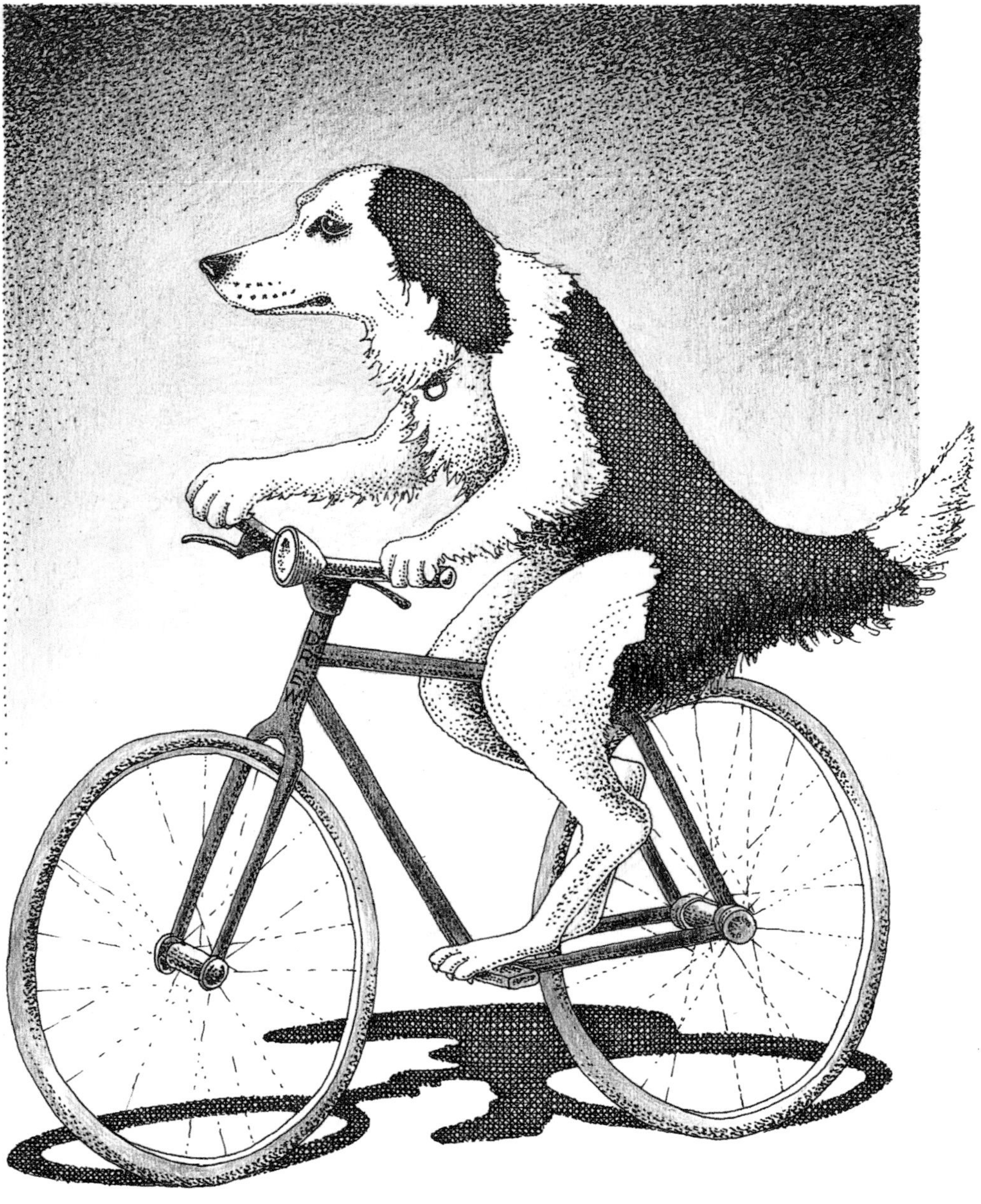

doggypedal

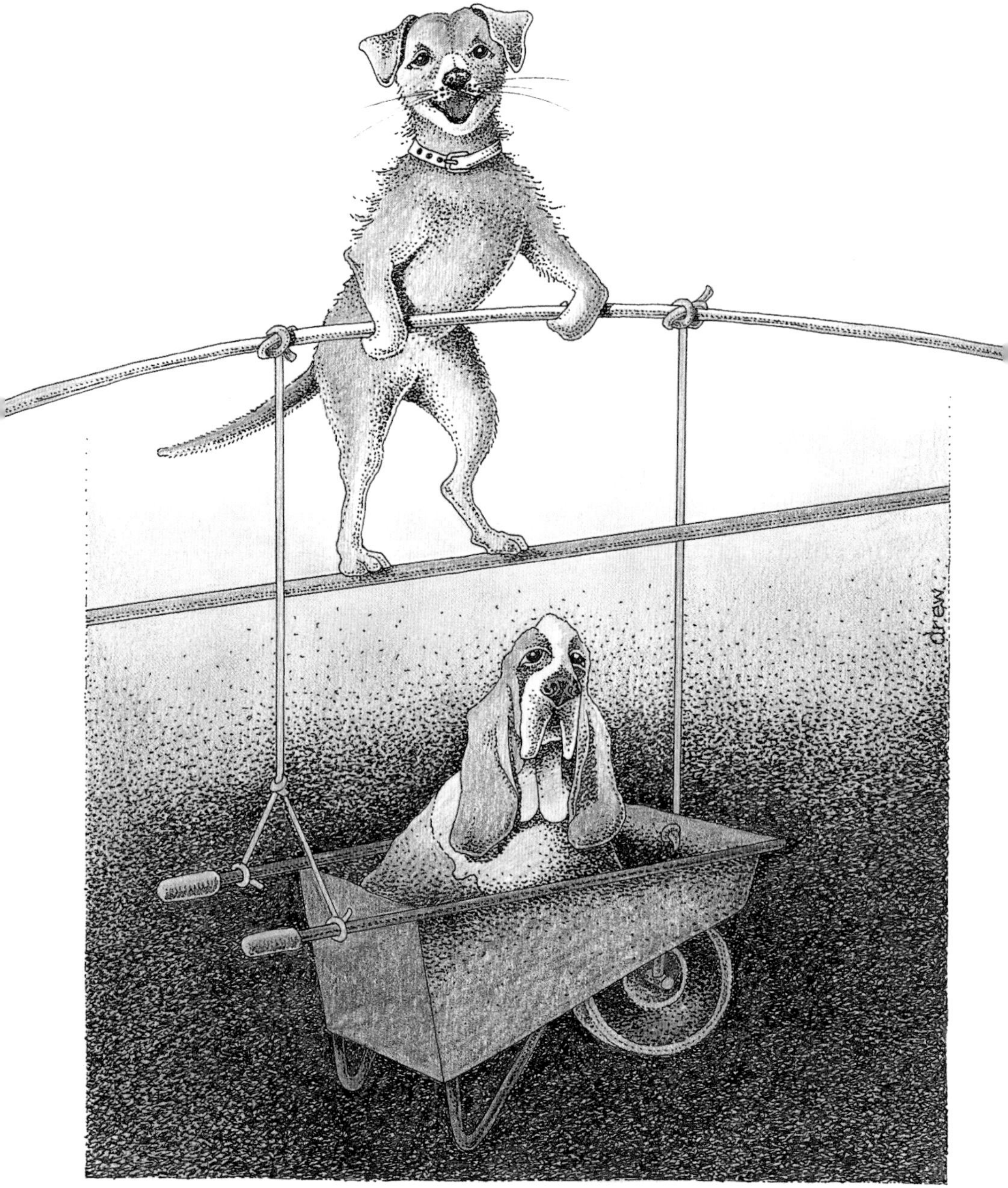
drew

dangerous dogs act

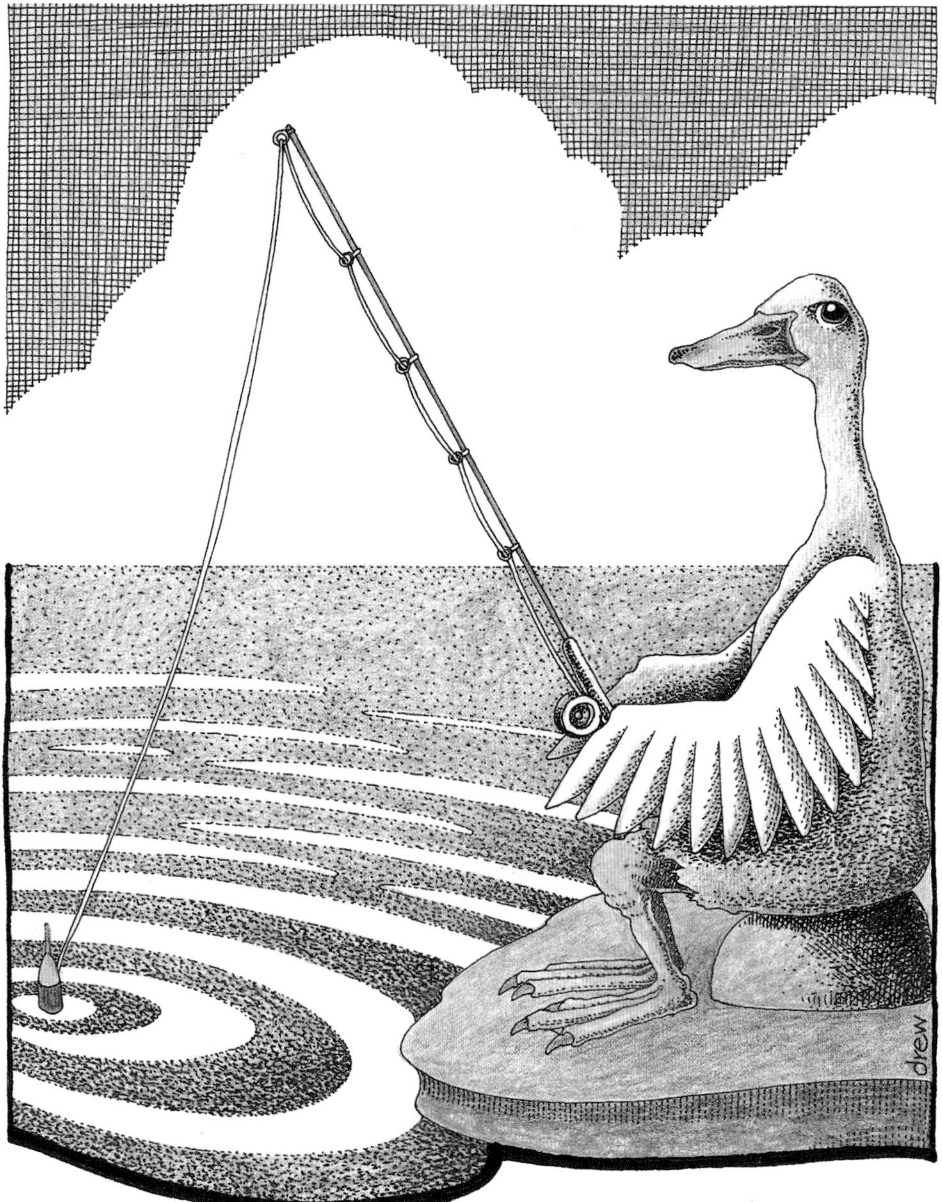
drew

There's a fine line between fishing and just standing on the shore like an idiot.
steven wright

An Incident near Basingstoke

Carefree and aimless
a runner duck appeared:
righteous pure and blameless
others thought it weird.
Leaving in a puff of smoke
it never said a word,
never did explain the joke,
elusive irksome bird.

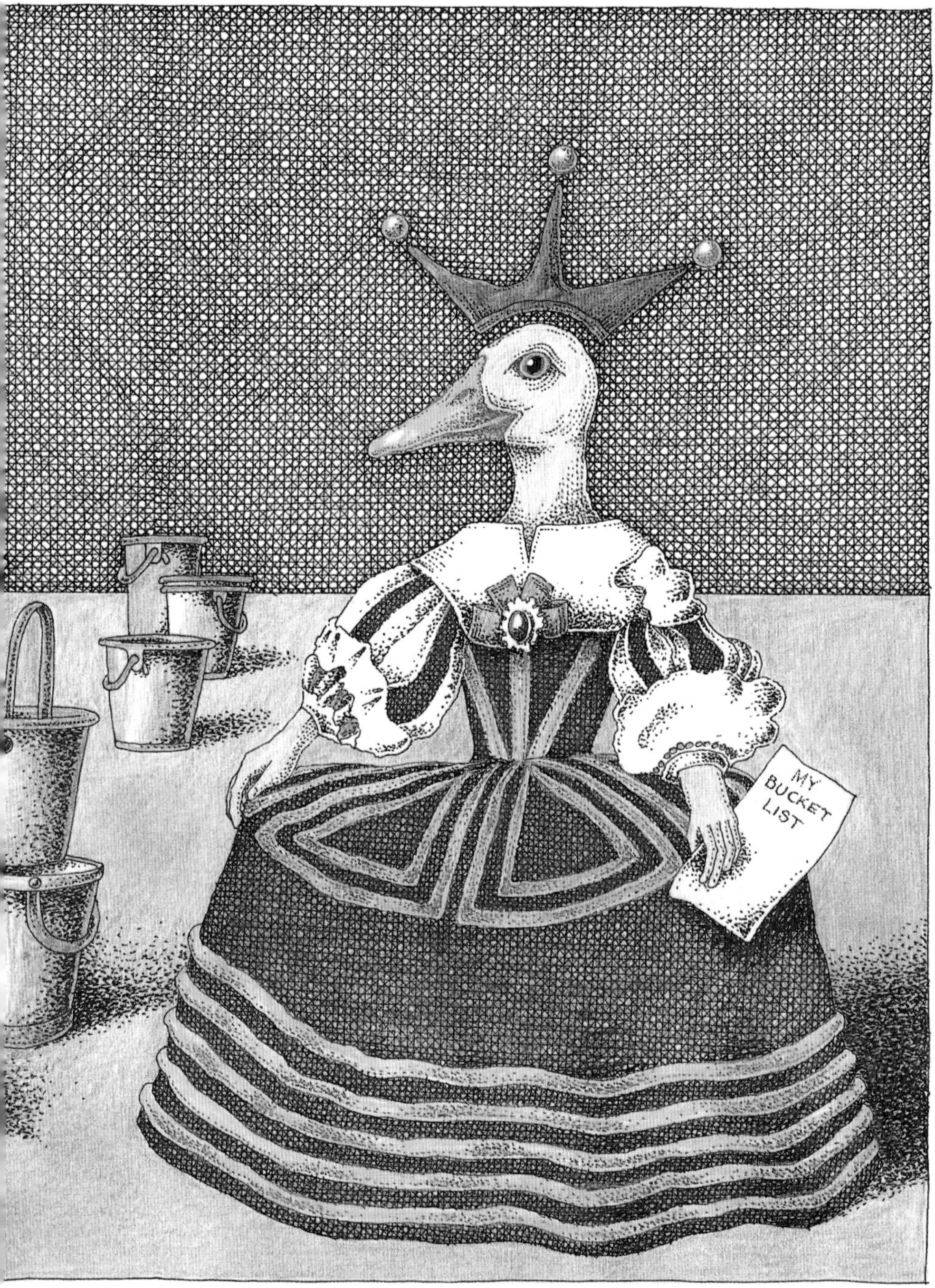
MY BUCKET LIST

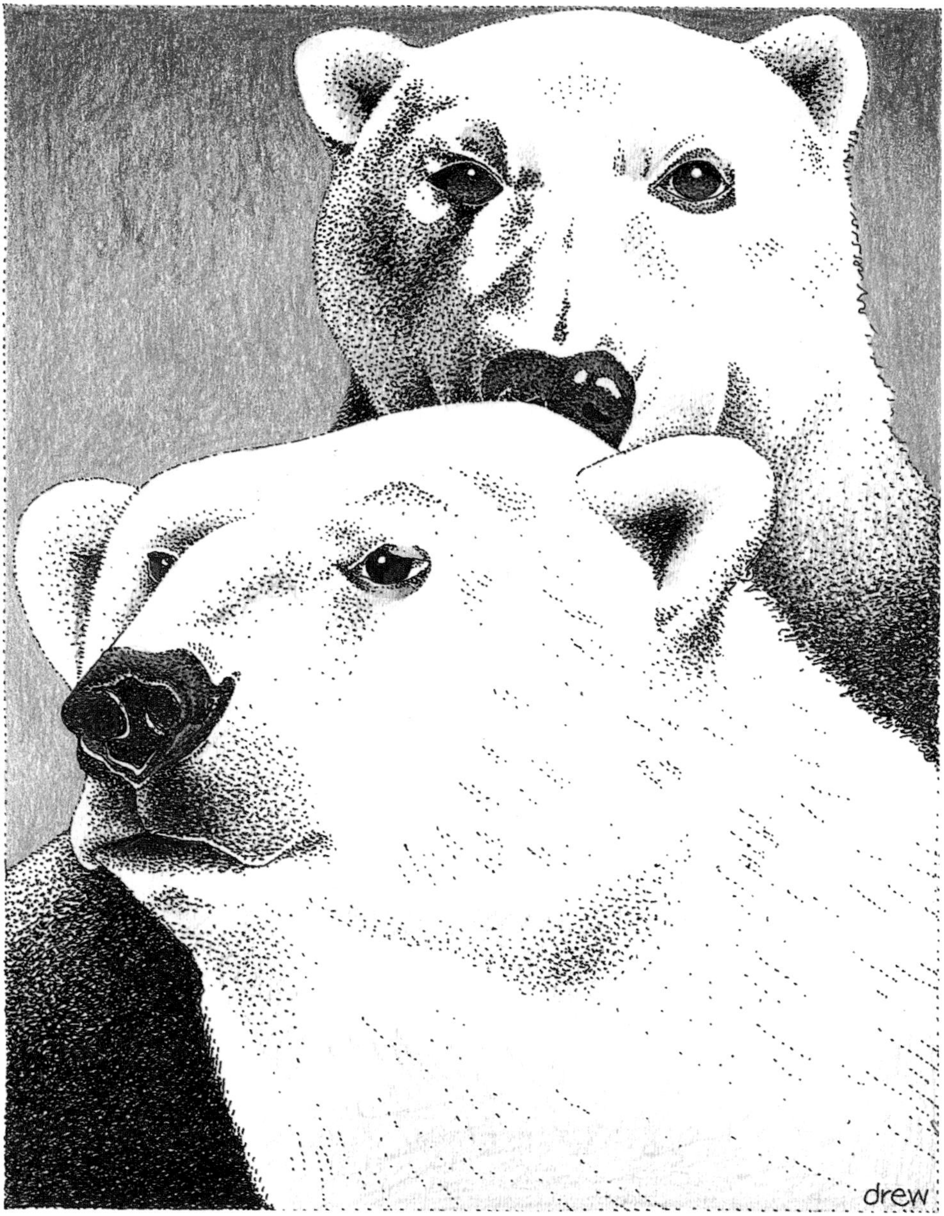
drew

bi - polar

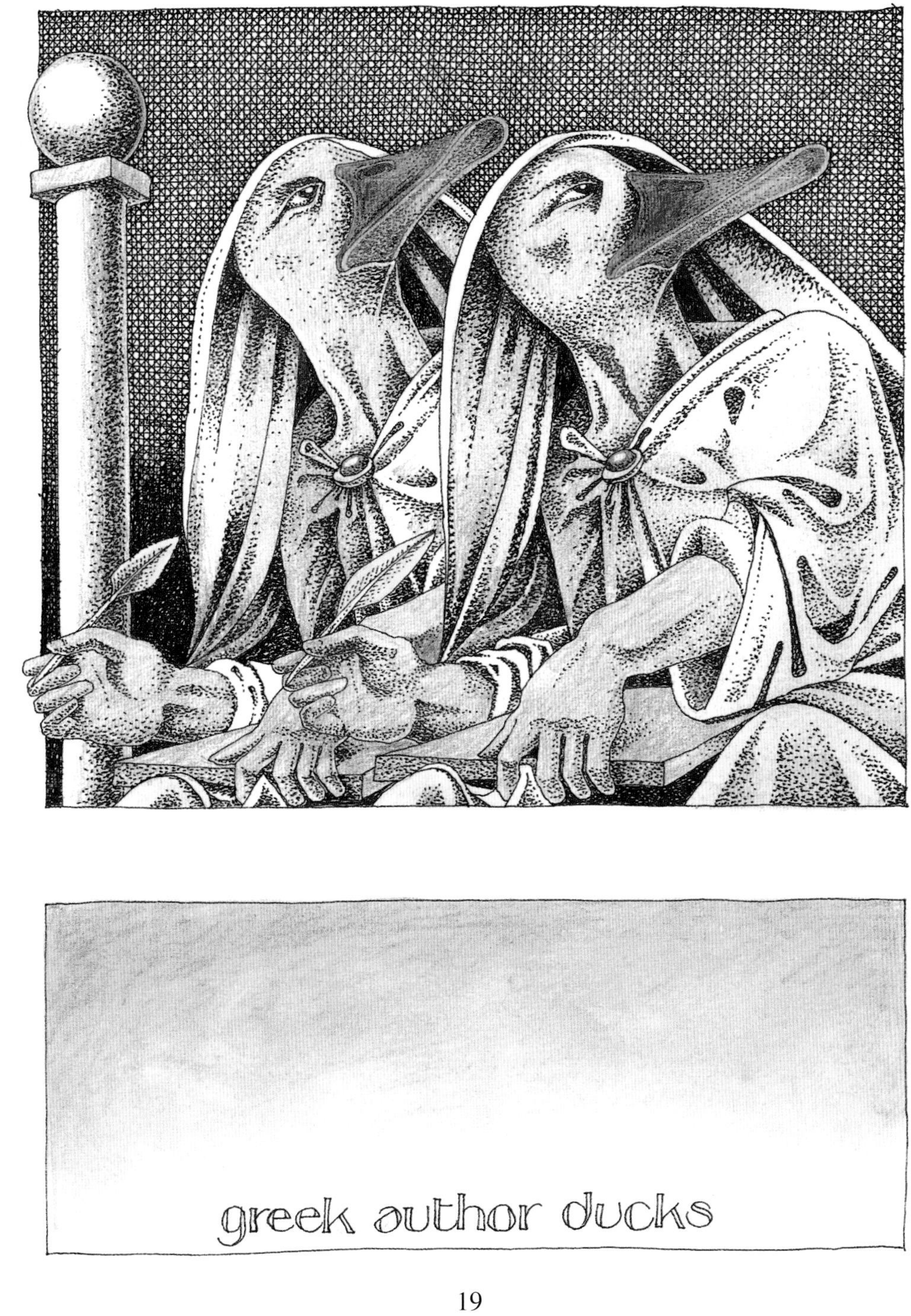

greek author ducks

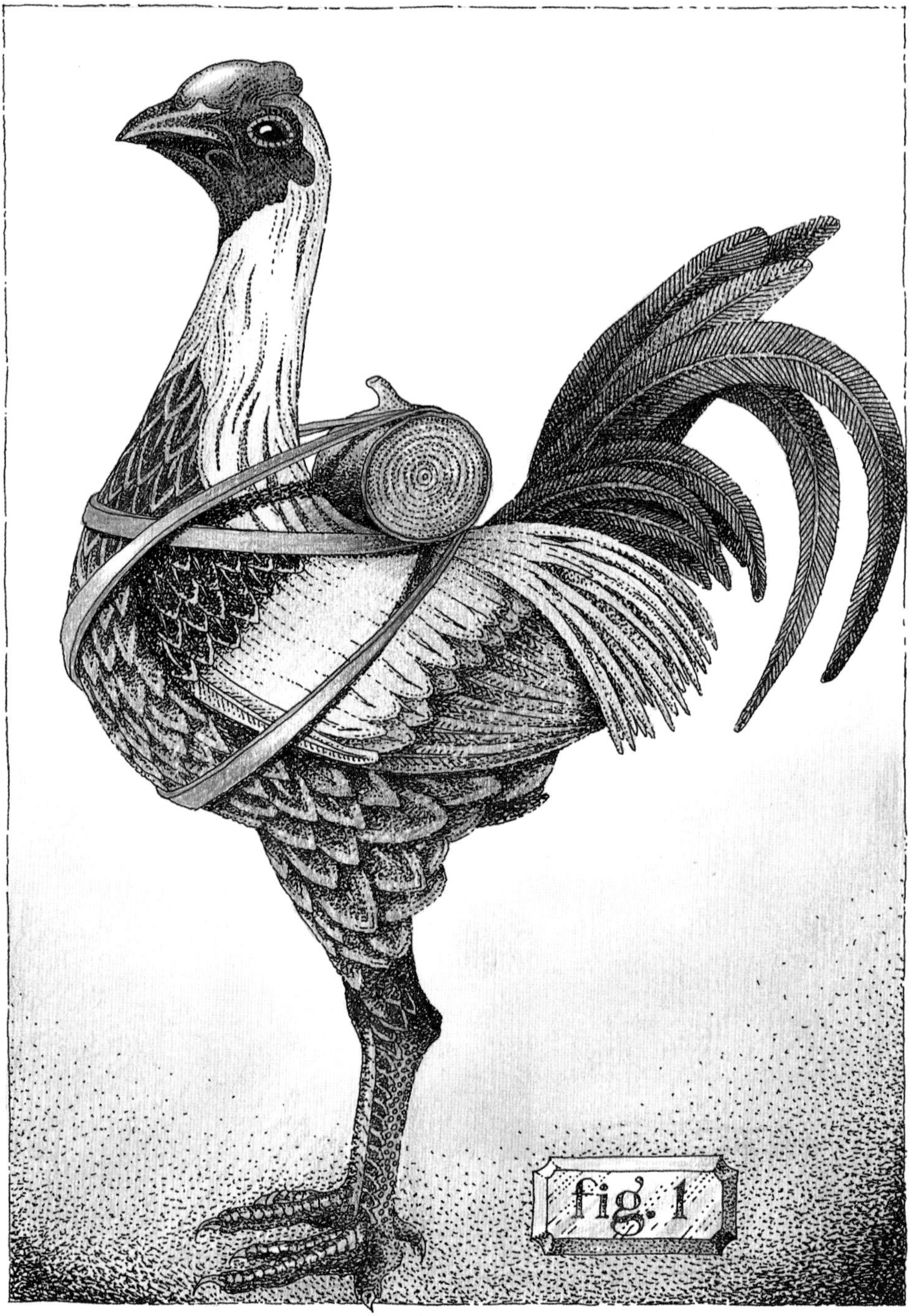
fig. 1

Advice for life

When your work is piling high –
if it starts to make you cry,
try a smile to blow away the frown.
If the jobs are overdue
try a glass of port or two :
never let a backlog get you down.

see fig. 1

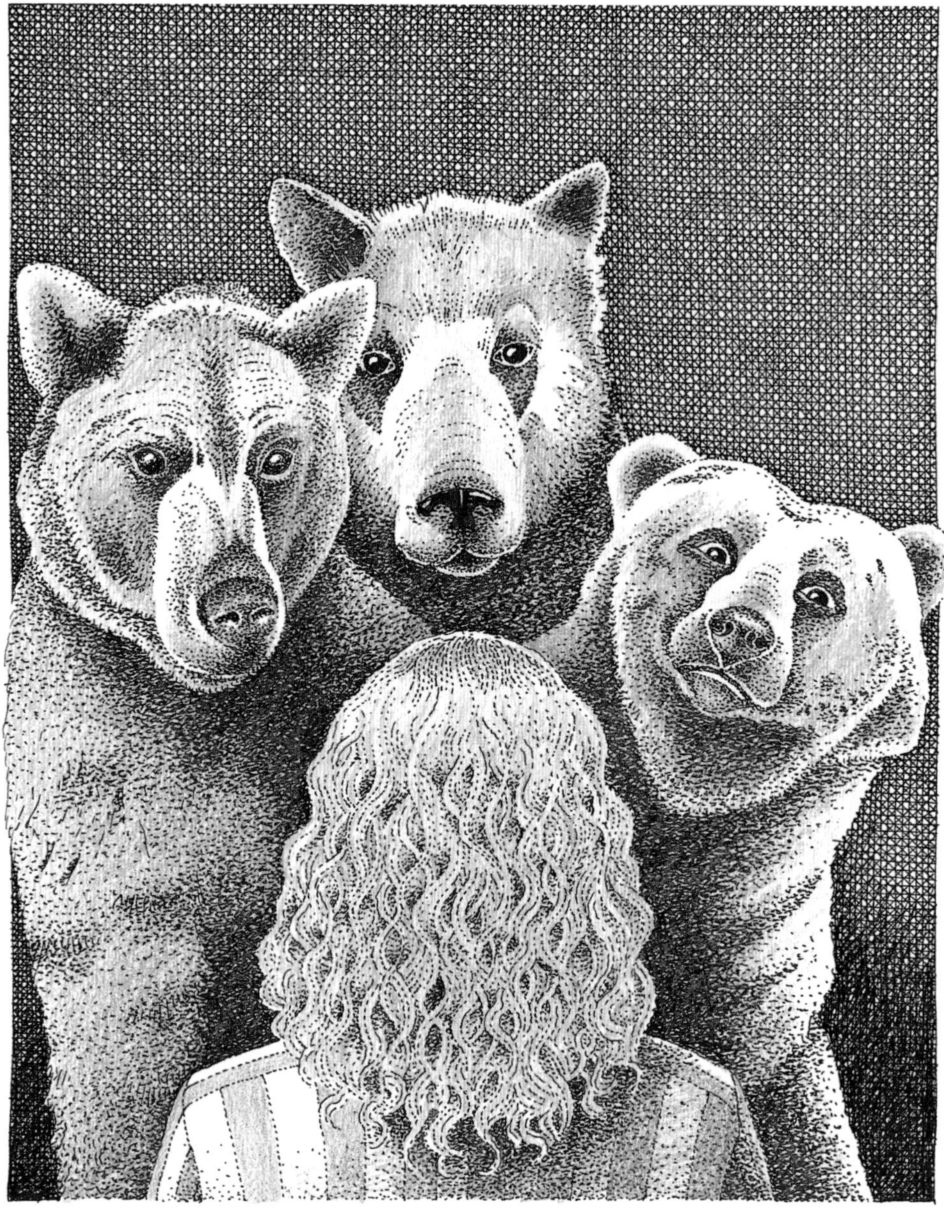

suddenly . . .
goldilocks realised
everything had gone bear-shaped.

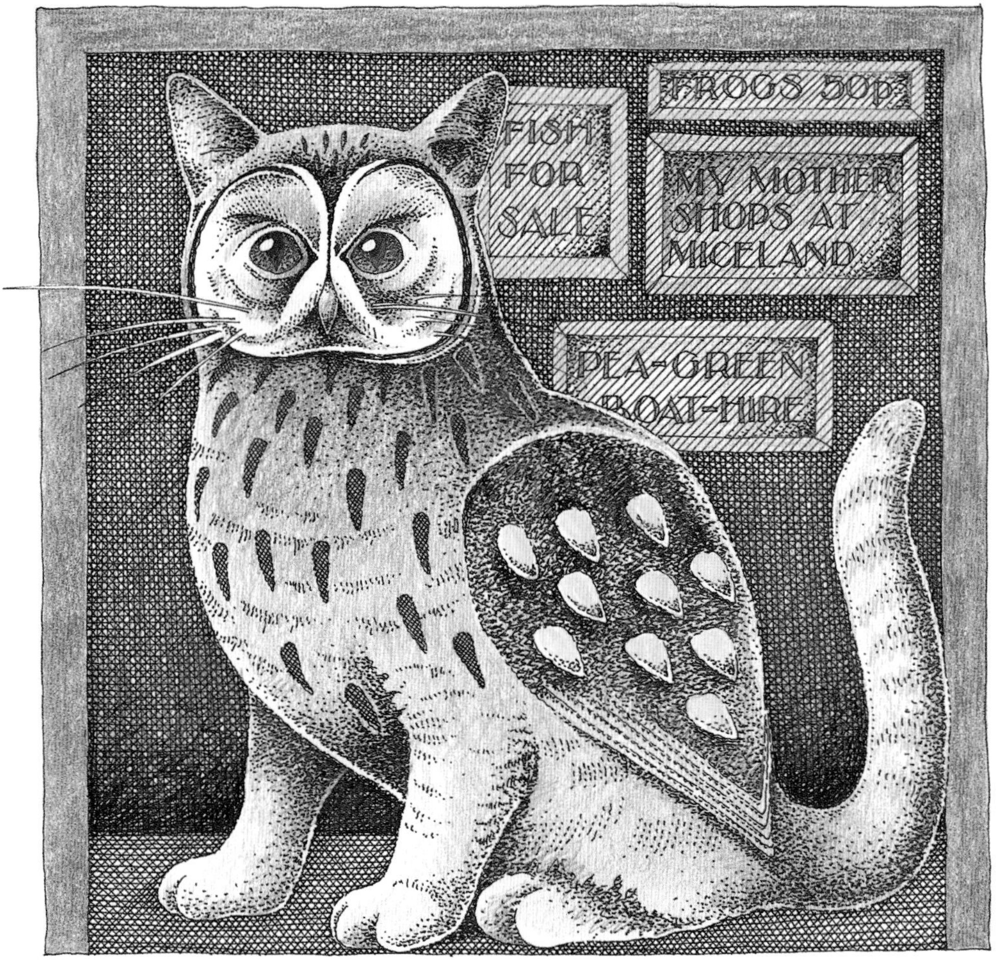
FROGS 50p
FISH FOR SALE
MY MOTHER SHOPS AT MICELAND
PEA-GREEN BOAT-HIRE

My mother was the pussycat.
My father was the owl.
The offspring posed before you here:
a schizophrenic fowl.
My favourite is a bowl of milk
directly from the cow.
You'll never find another beast
who cries 'toowit-meow'.

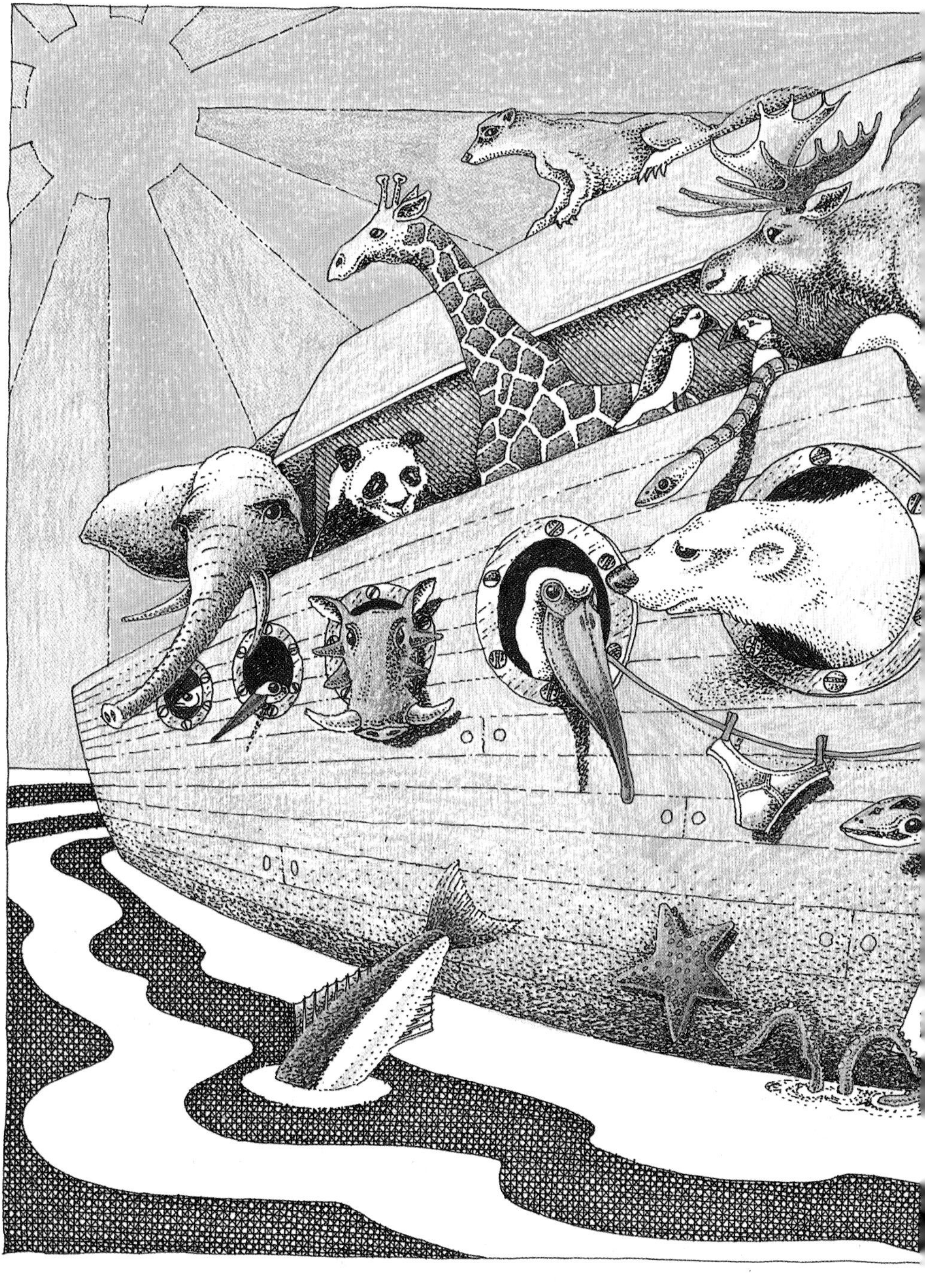

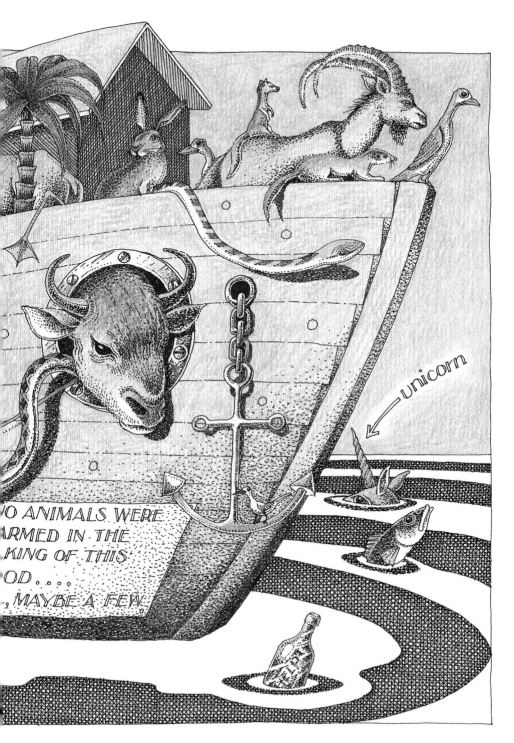

unicorn

O ANIMALS WERE
ARMED IN THE
KING OF THIS
OD....
MAYBE A FEW

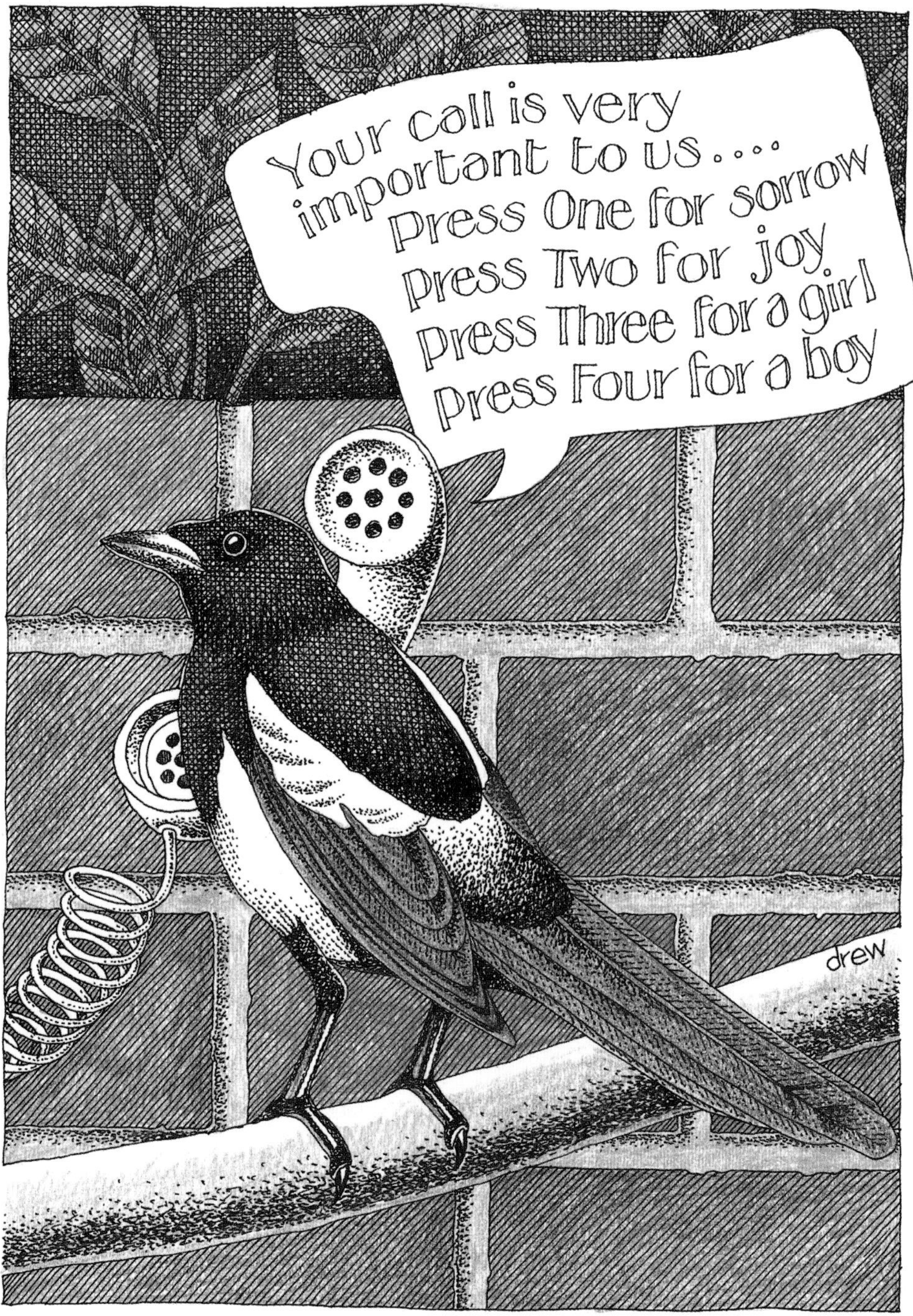
Your call is very important to us....
Press One for sorrow
Press Two for joy
Press Three for a girl
Press Four for a boy
drew

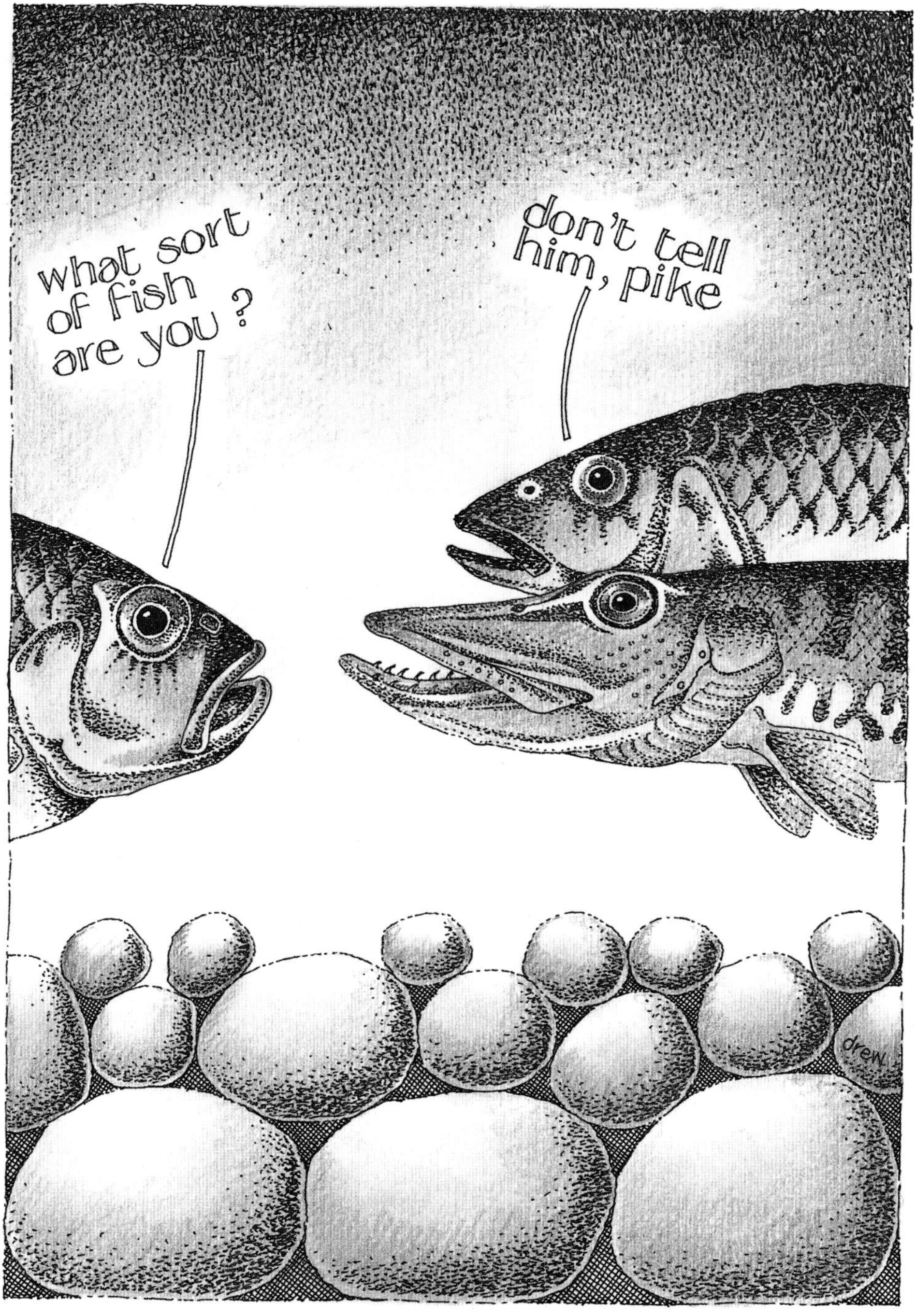
what sort of fish are you ?
don't tell him, pike
drew

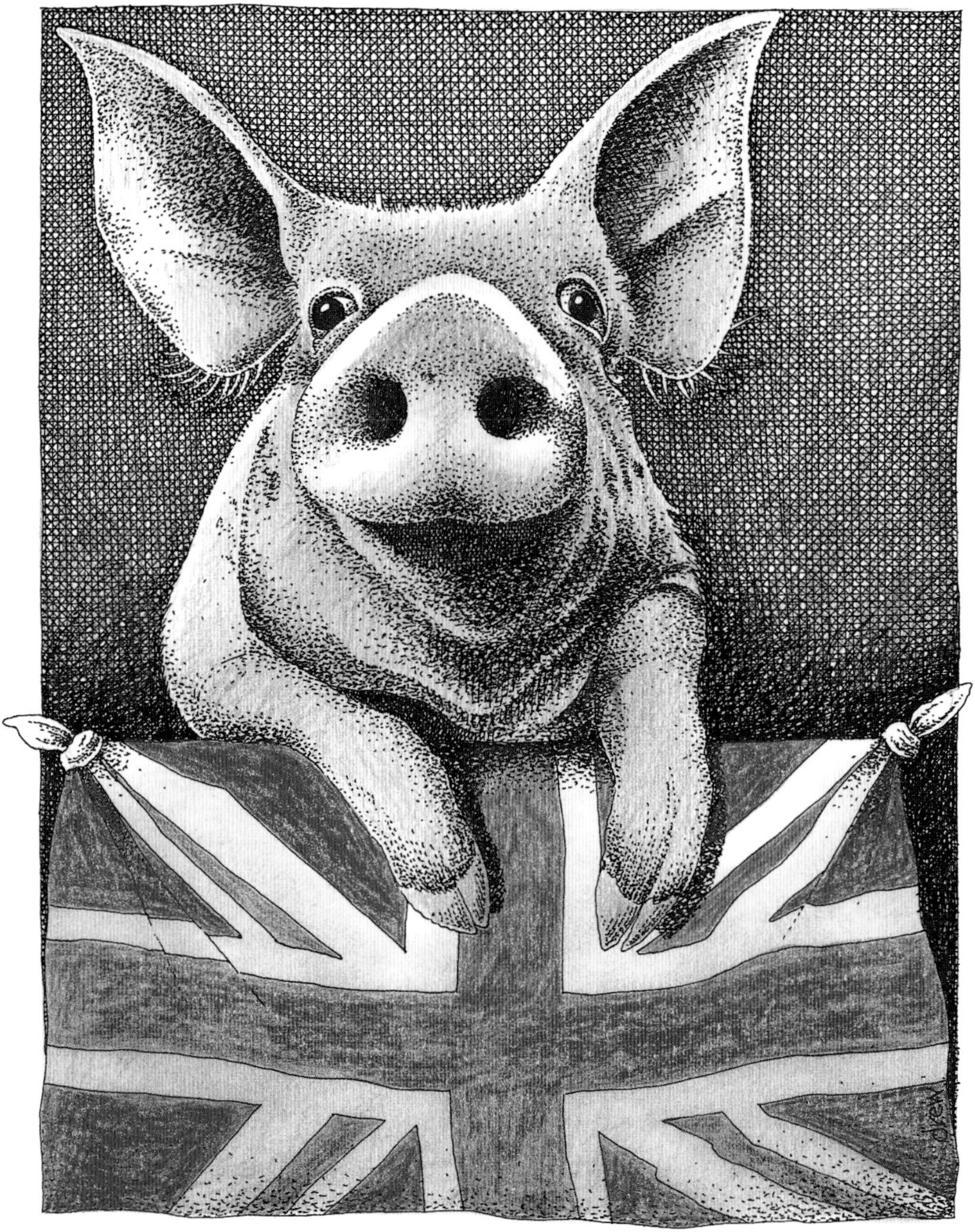

pig for victory

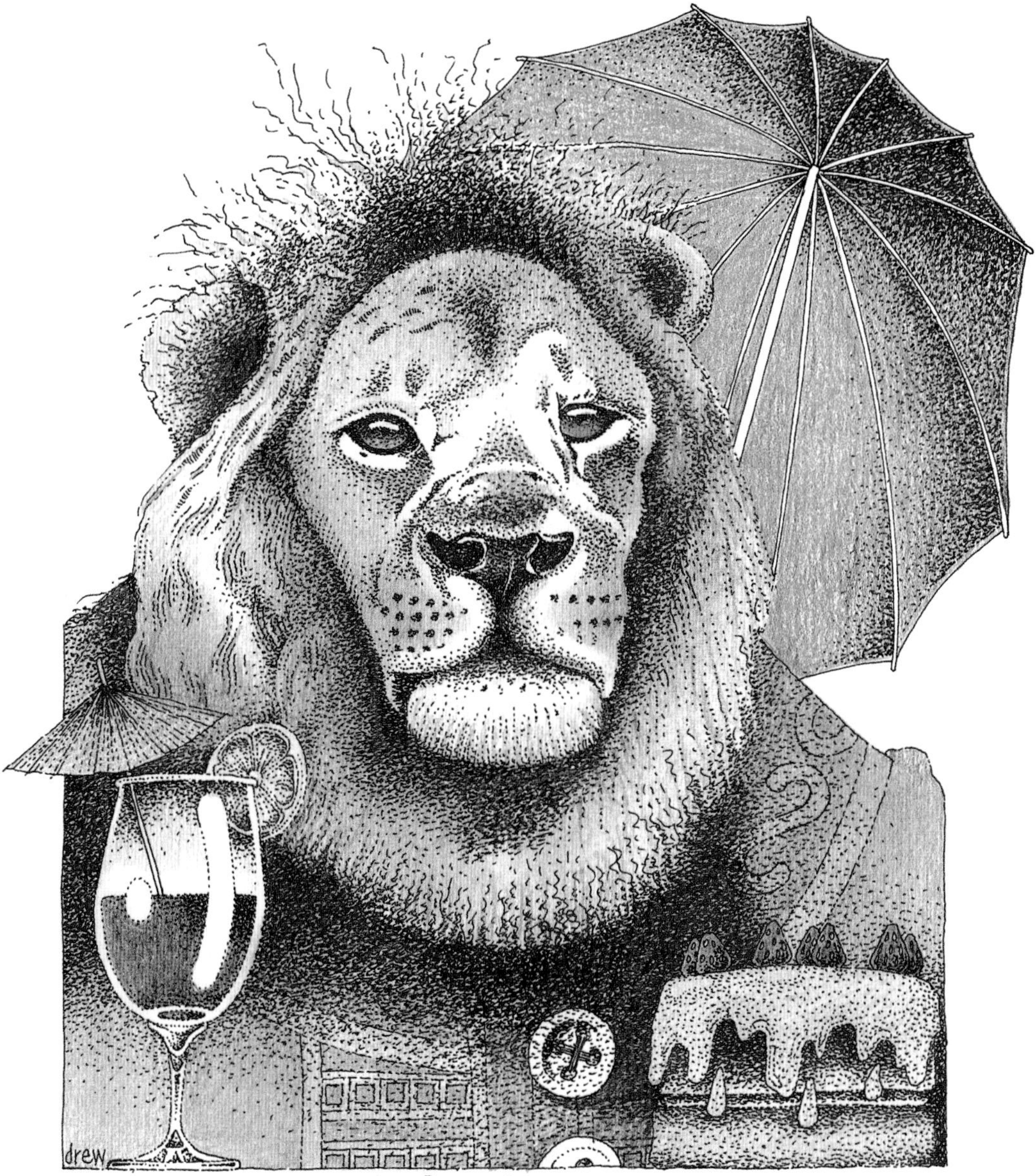
drew

I was perfectly happy
until someone said:
don't worry.

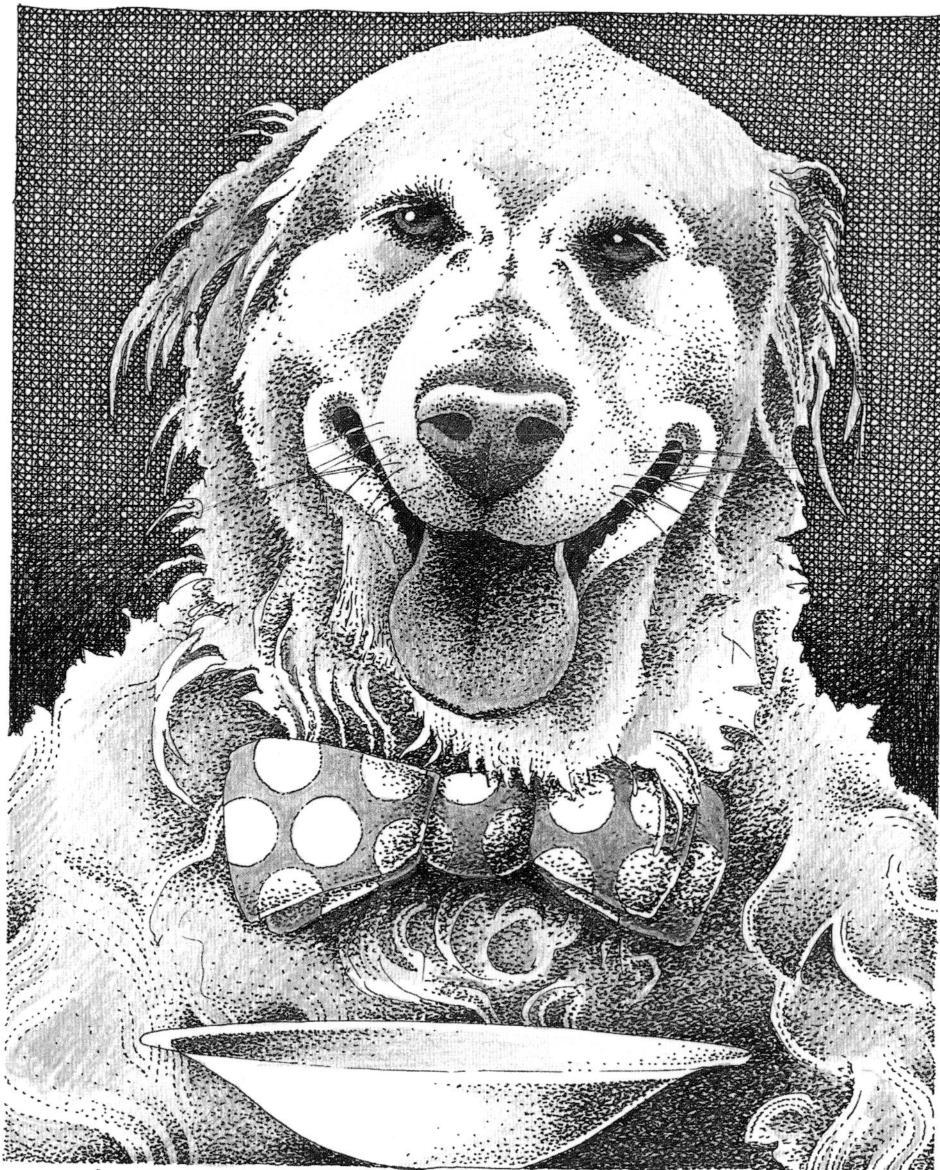

It is a truth universally acknowledged, that a hungry dog in possession of an empty bowl, must be in want of a bone.

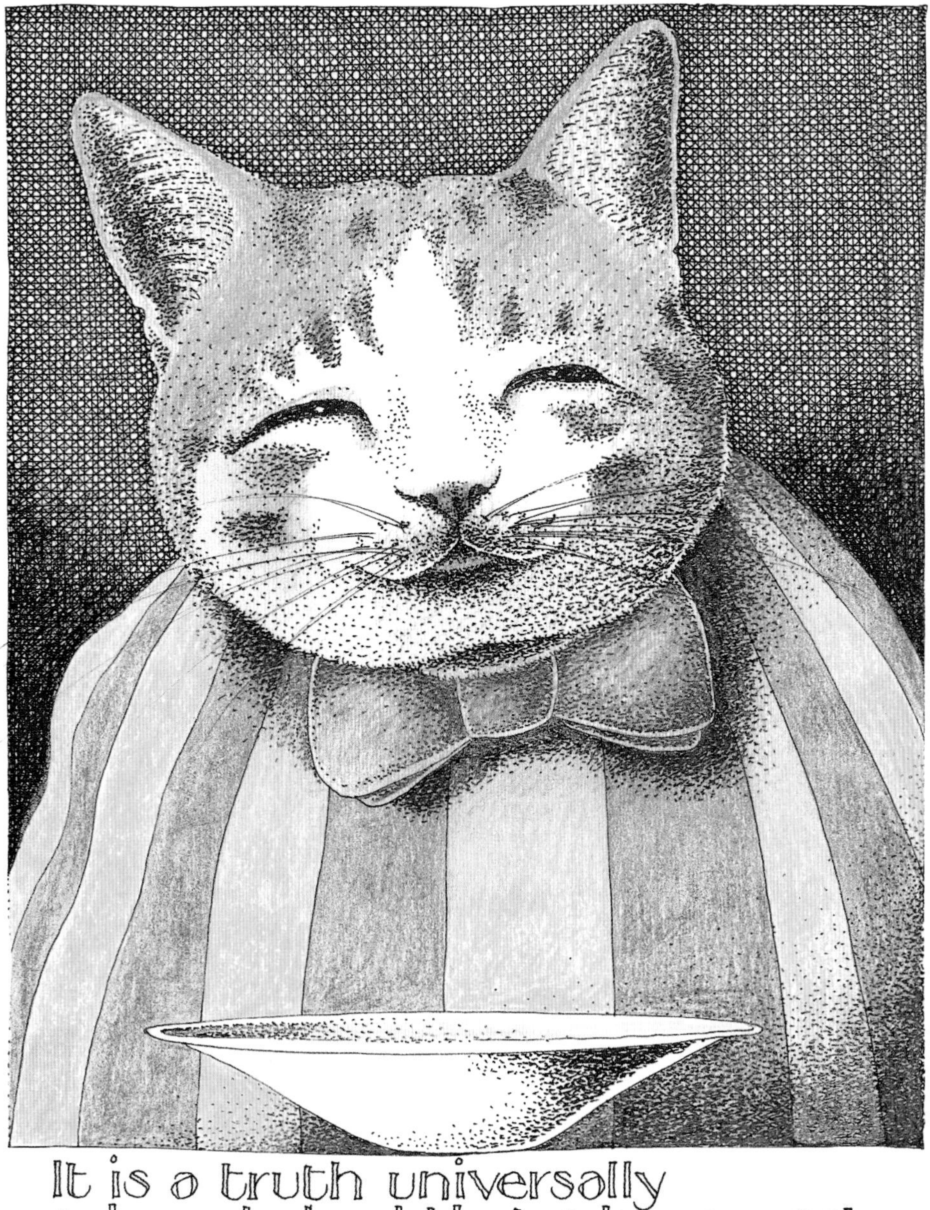

It is a truth universally acknowledged, that a hungry cat in possession of an empty bowl, must be in want of cream.

a scientific analysis of EQUINE TYPES

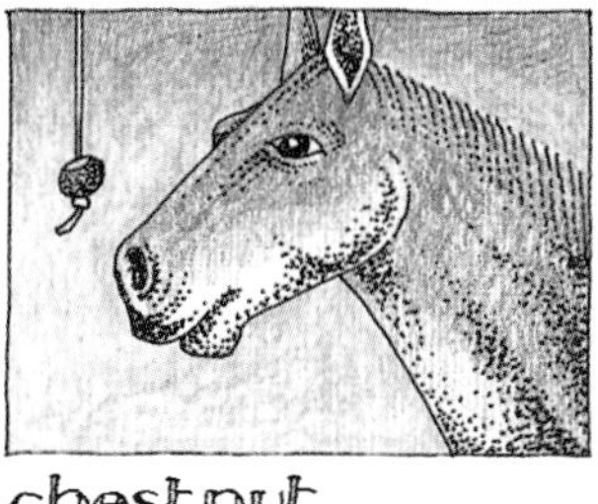

chestnut horse

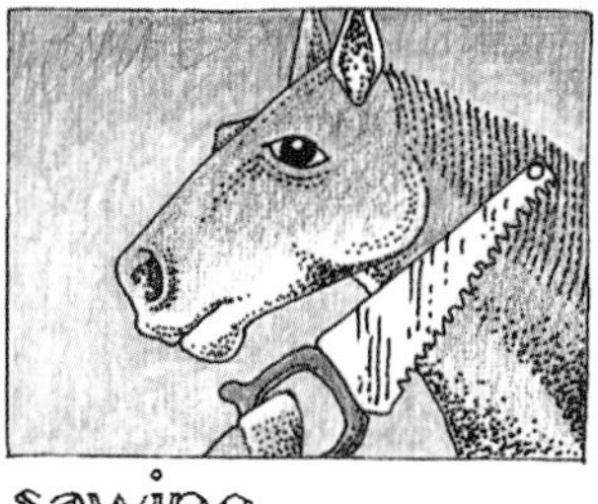

sawing horse

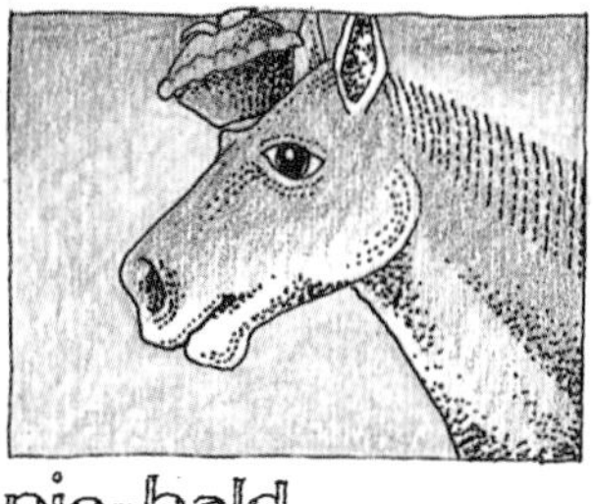

pie-bald horse

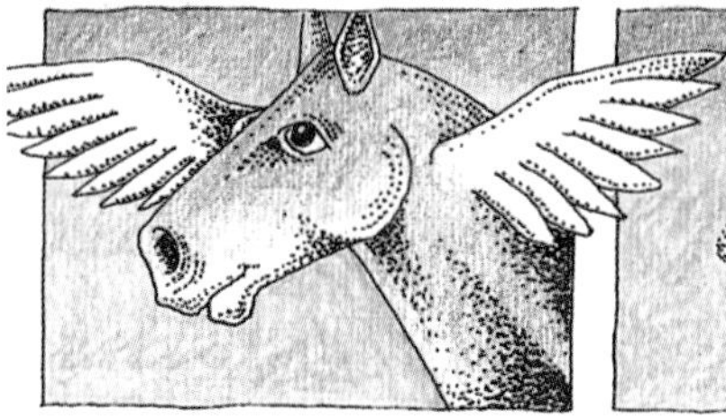

horse fly

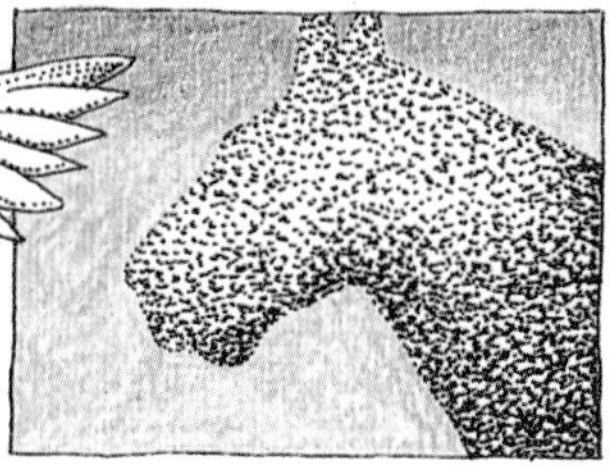

grey

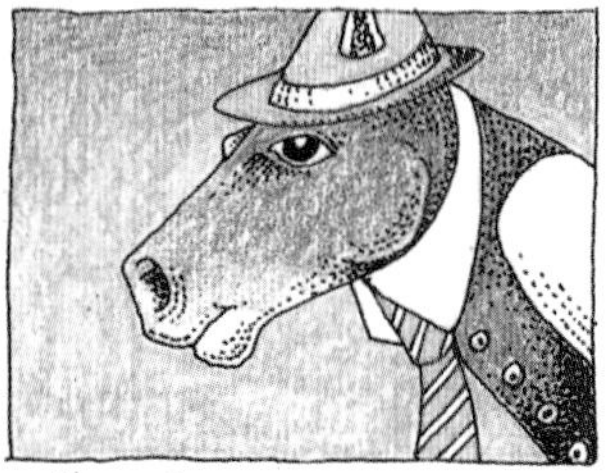

clothes horse

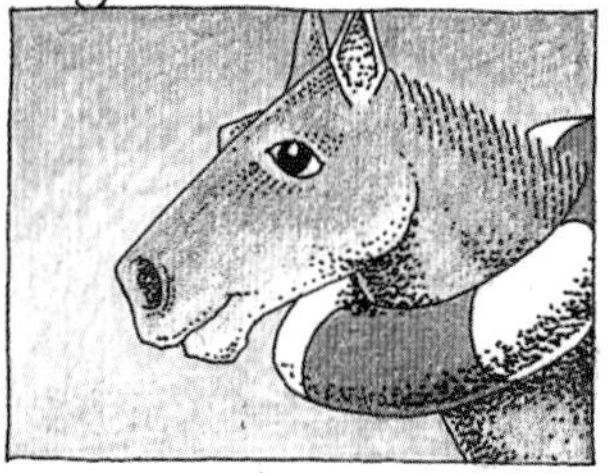

sea horse

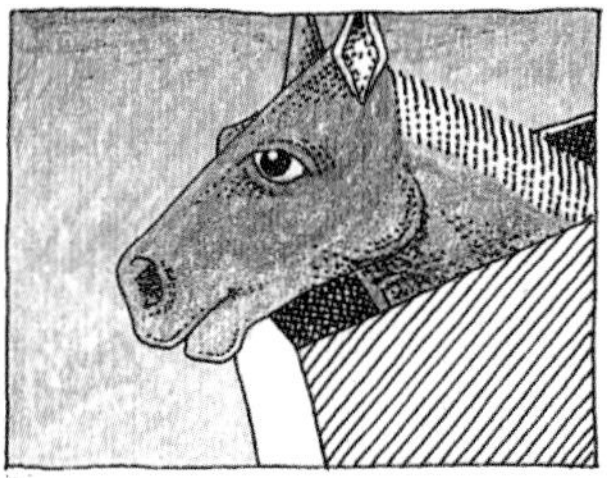

horse box

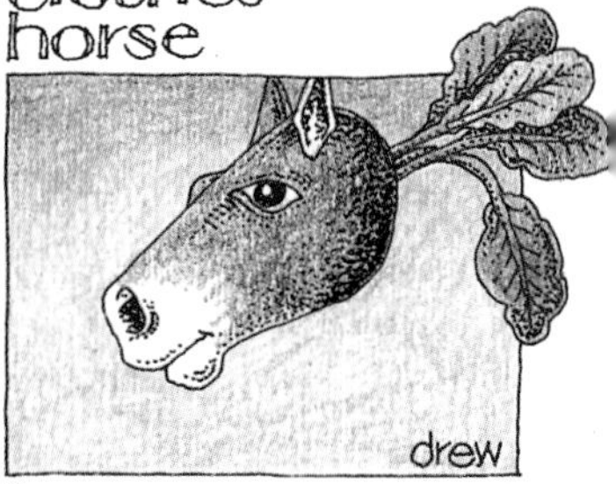
drew

horse radish

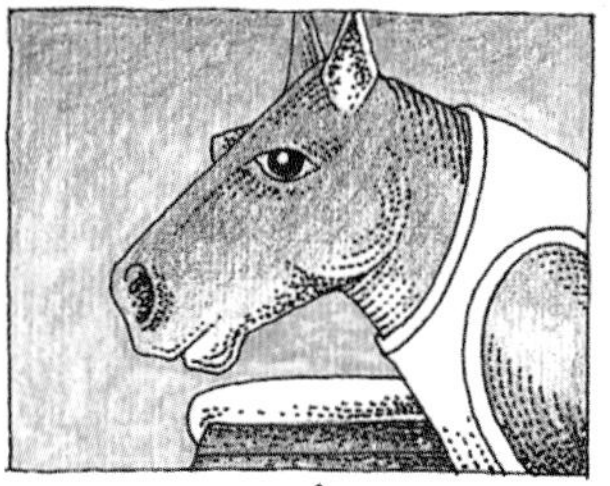

gymnasium horse

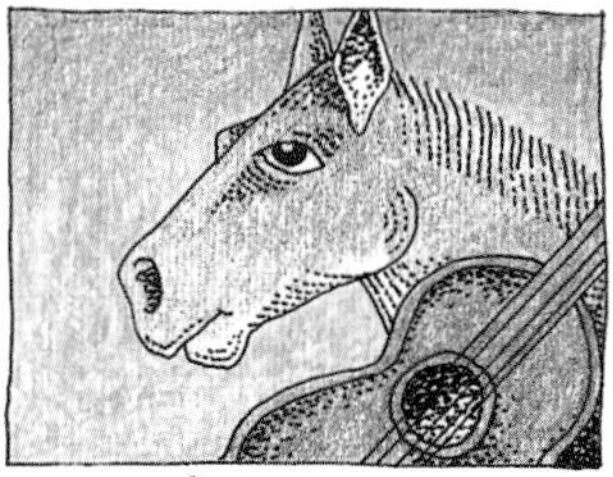

rocking horse

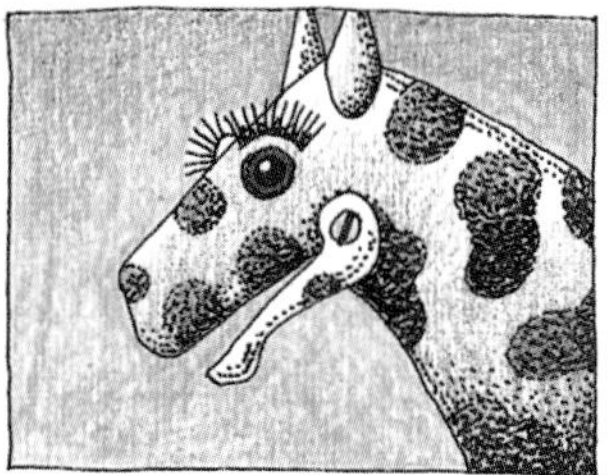

pantomime horse

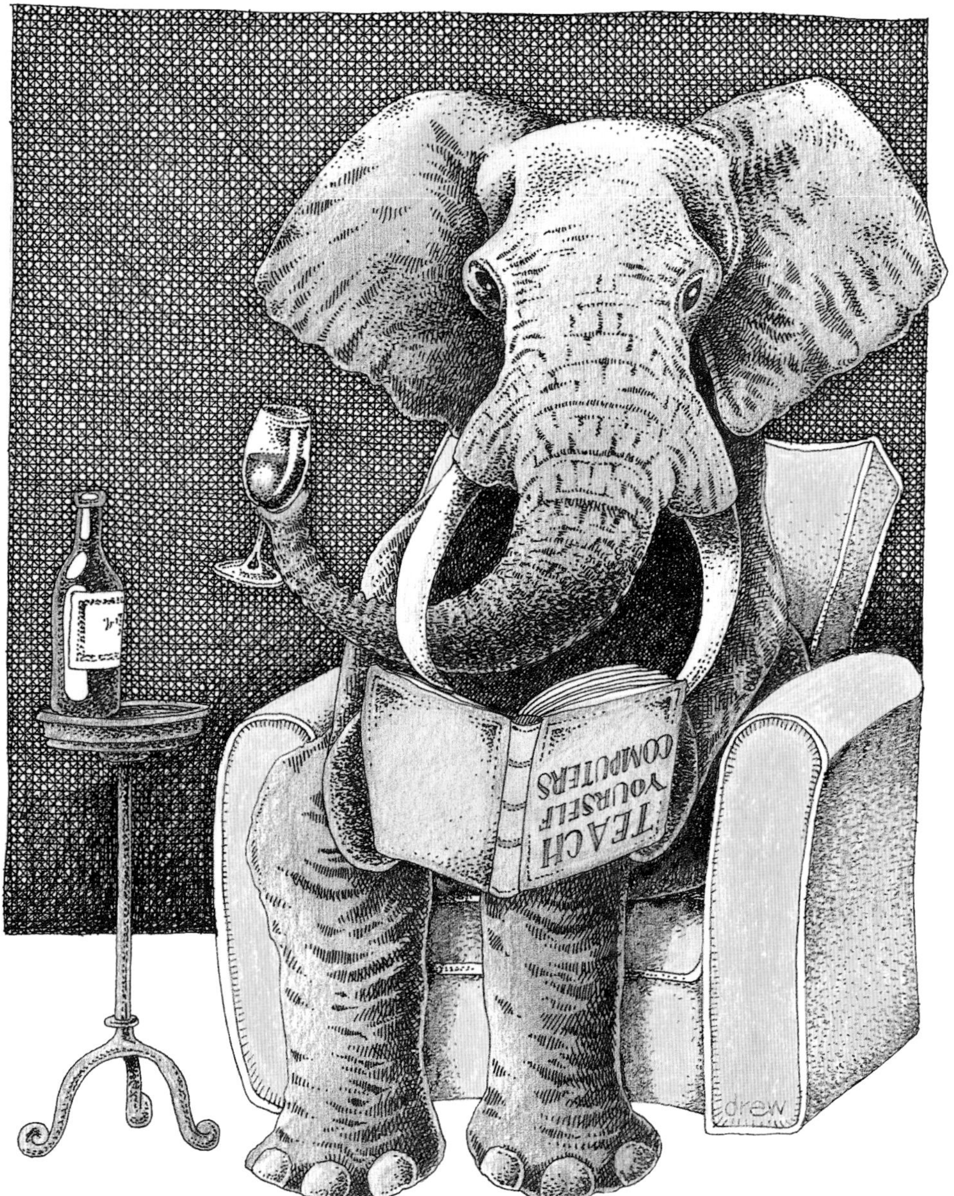
TEACH YOURSELF COMPUTERS
drew

By the time you reach old age
you've learned everything.
Unfortunately you can't remember
any of it.

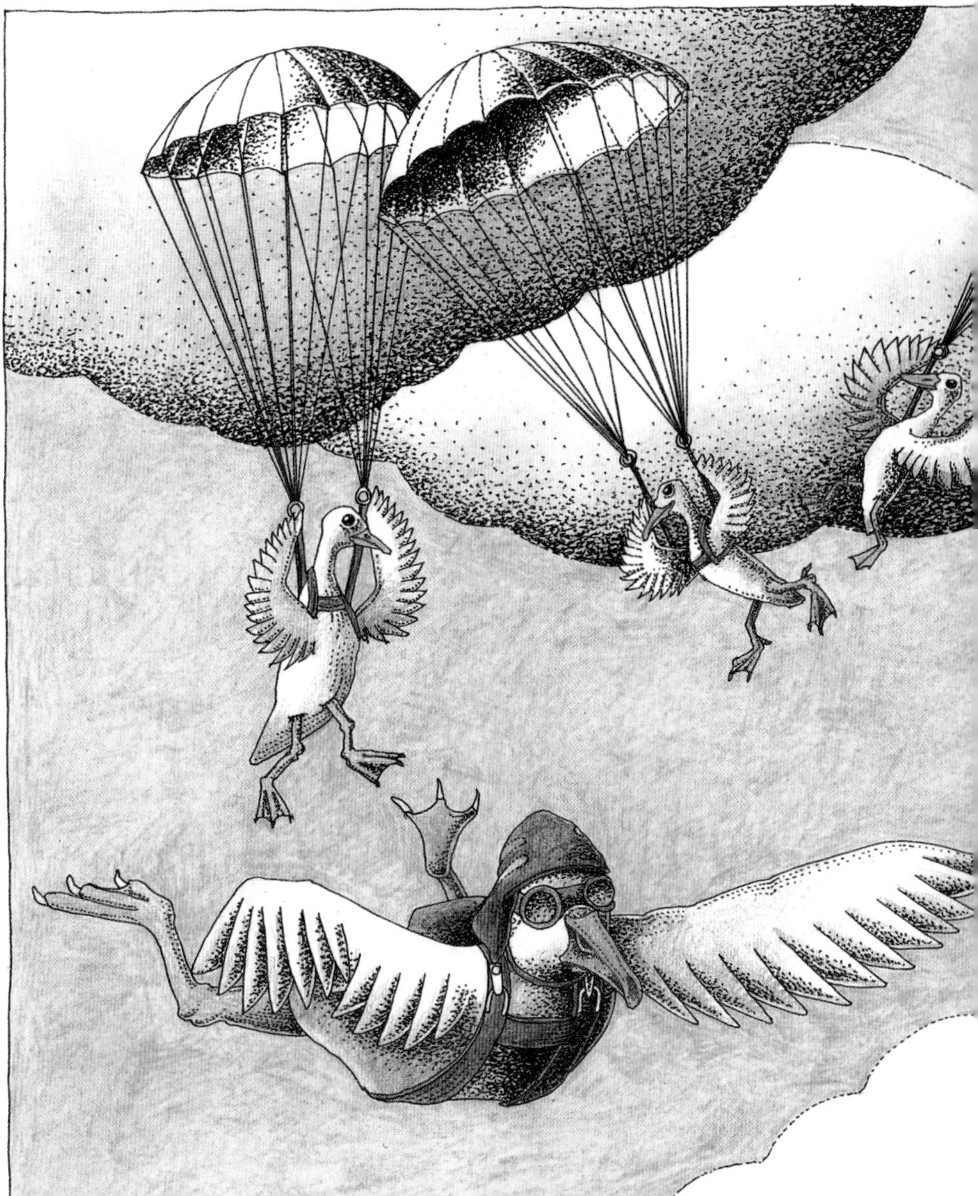

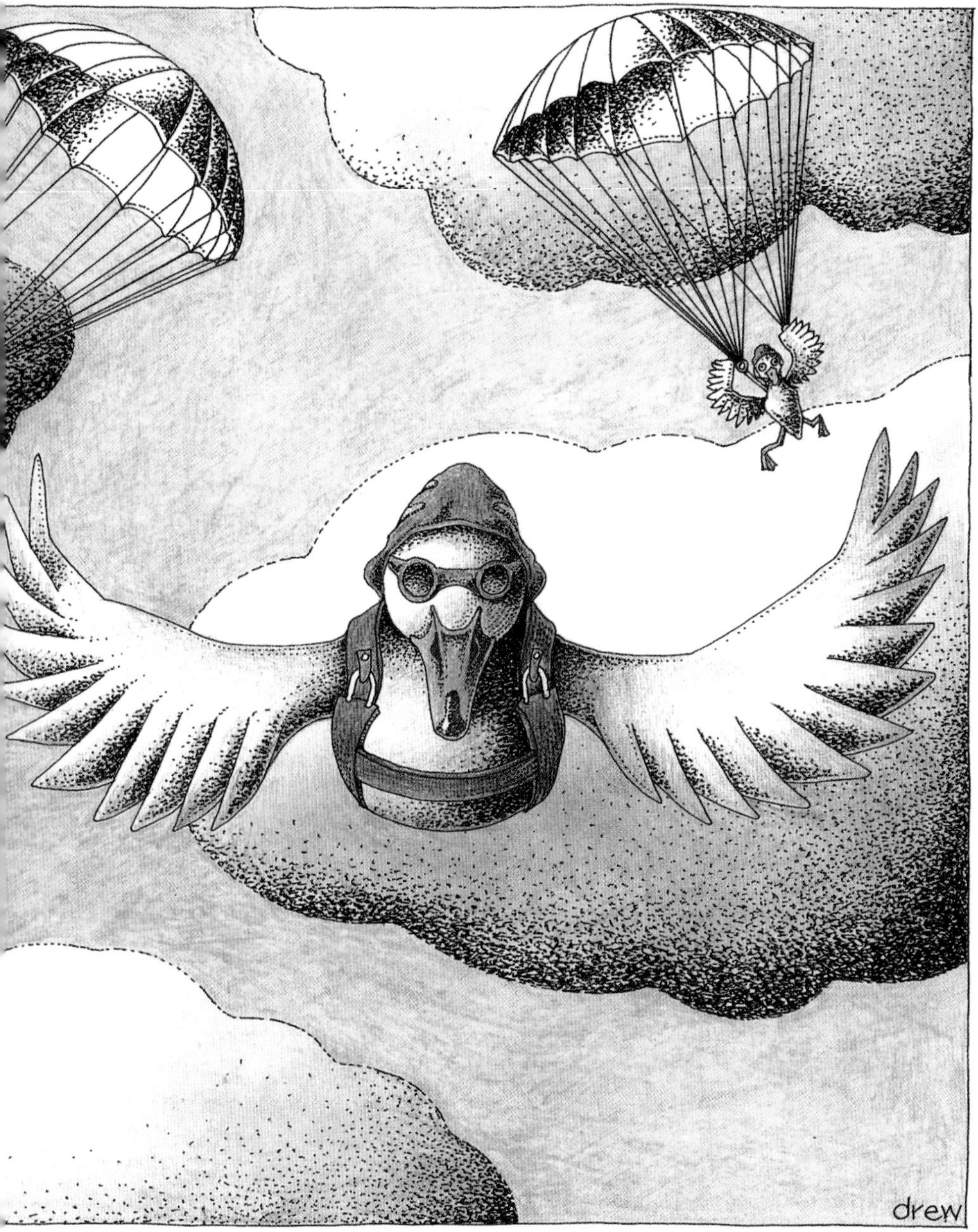
drew

you don't need a parachute to skydive:
you only need a parachute to skydive twice.

OPTIMISM

You can't touch a rainbow
    without feeling blue.
You can't join a party
    without superglue.
You can't smoke a herring
    without seeing red.
You can't make a kipper
    return from the dead.
You can't drain a bottle
    without tasting dregs.
You can't make an umlaut "
    without breaking legs.

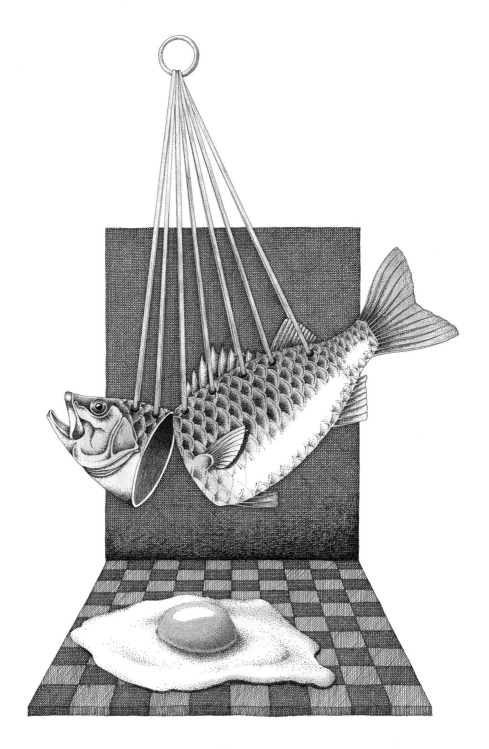

SPOT THE LONDON UNDERGROUND STATION:

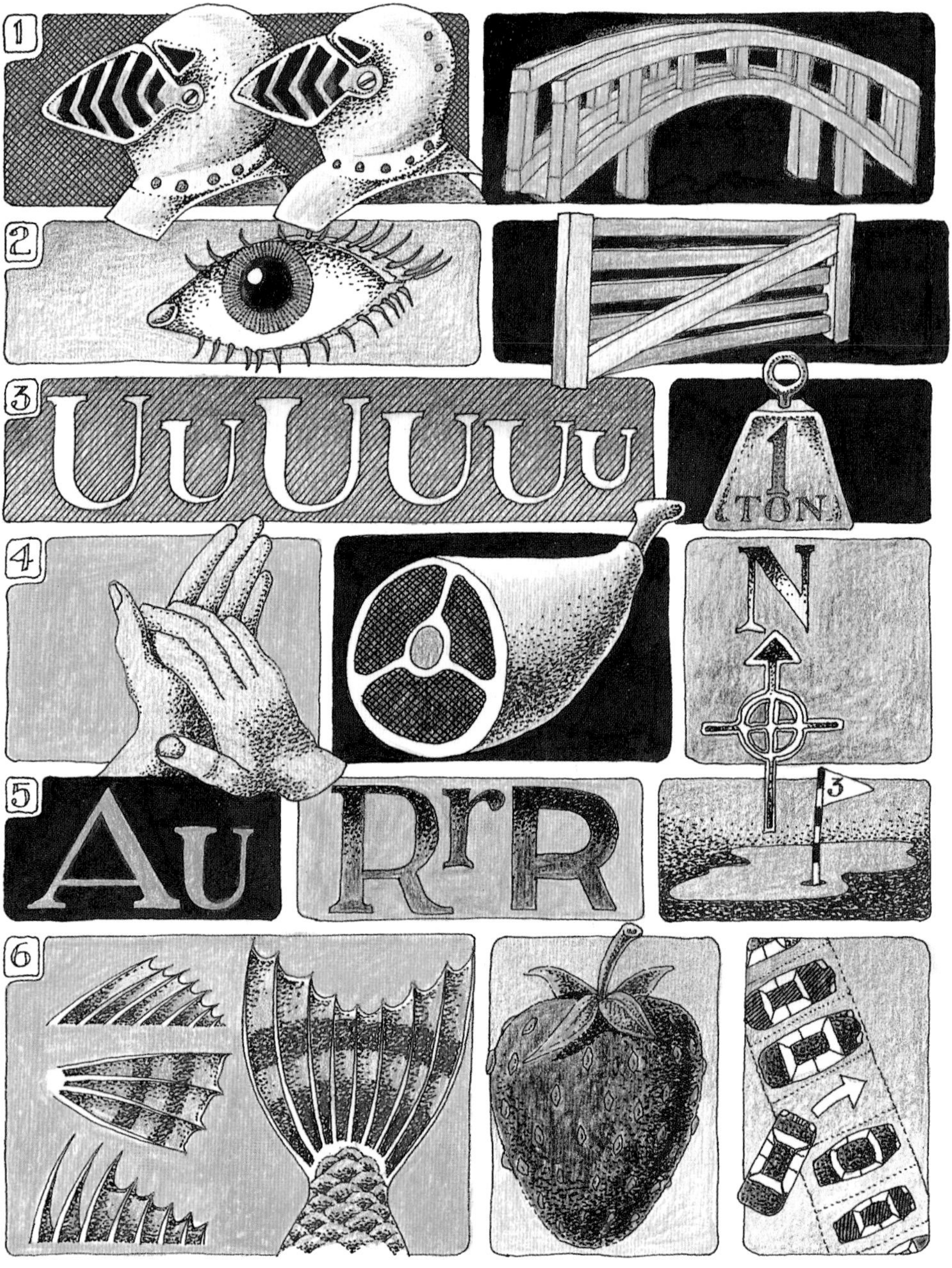
1
2
3
UuUUUu
1
TON
4
N
5
Au
RrR
3
6

SPOT THE LONDON UNDERGROUND STATION:

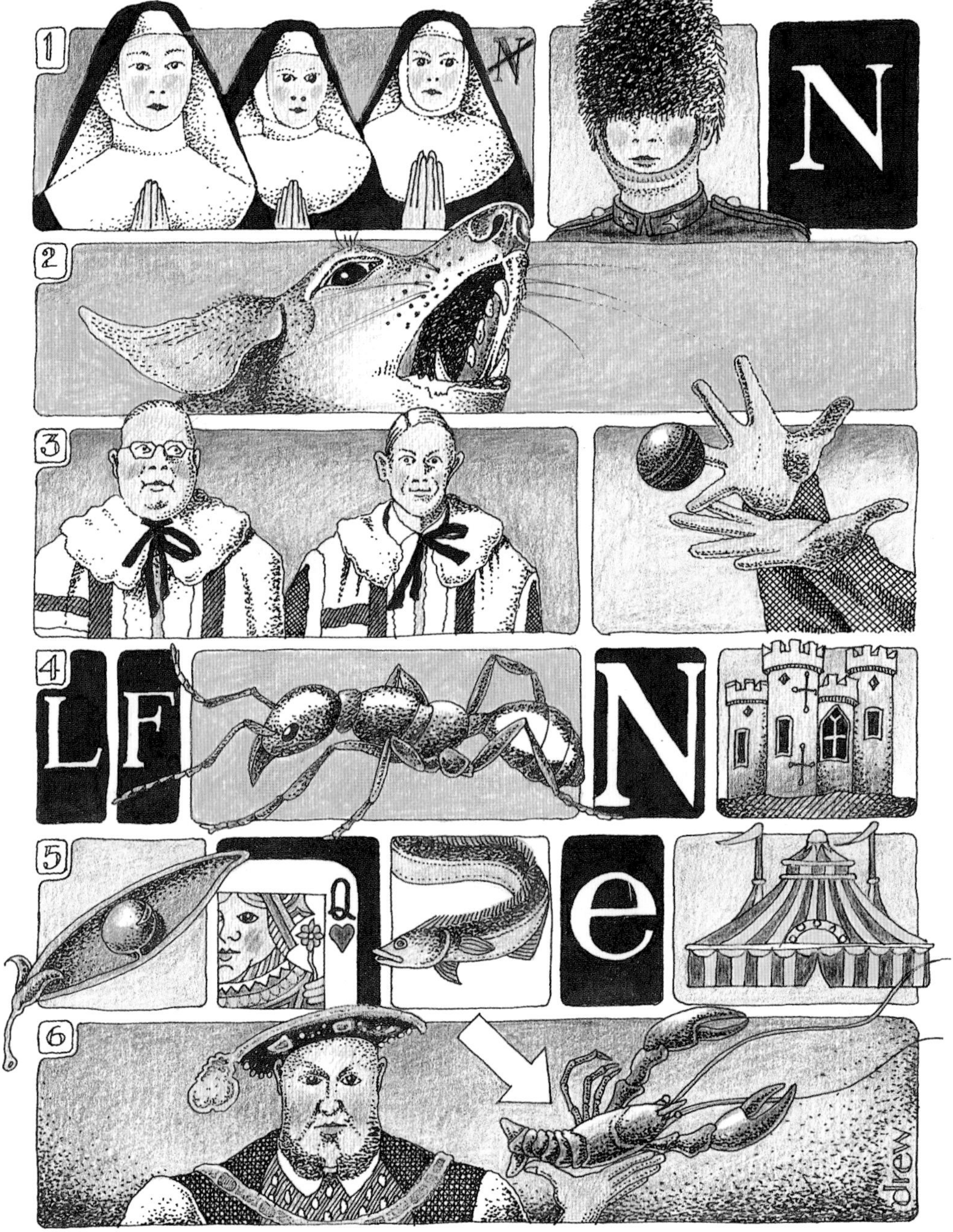

1
N
N
2
3
4
L
F
N
5
Q
e
6
drew

from Ealing down to Dover (

Scarfell Pike and Musselburg'

cks: and Lingfield, if you wish,

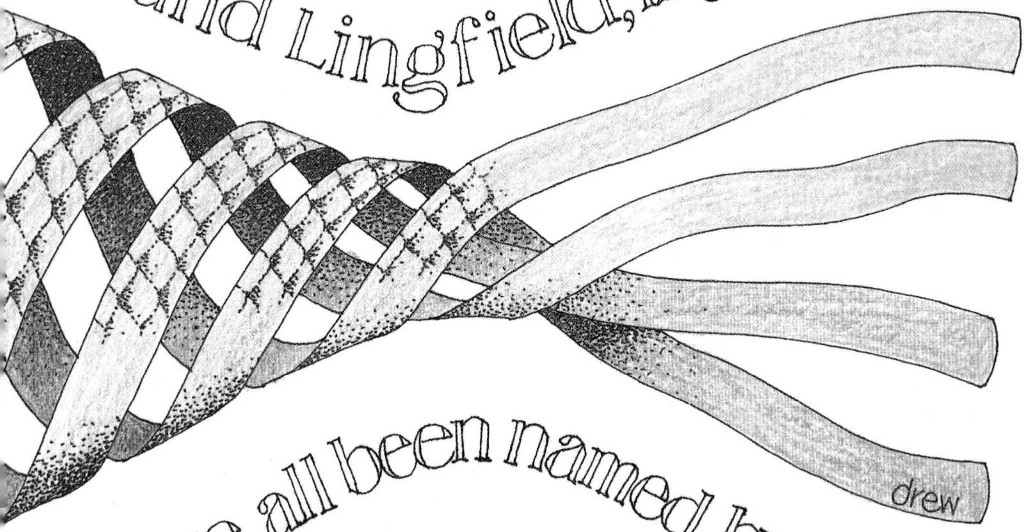
drew

they've all been named by fish

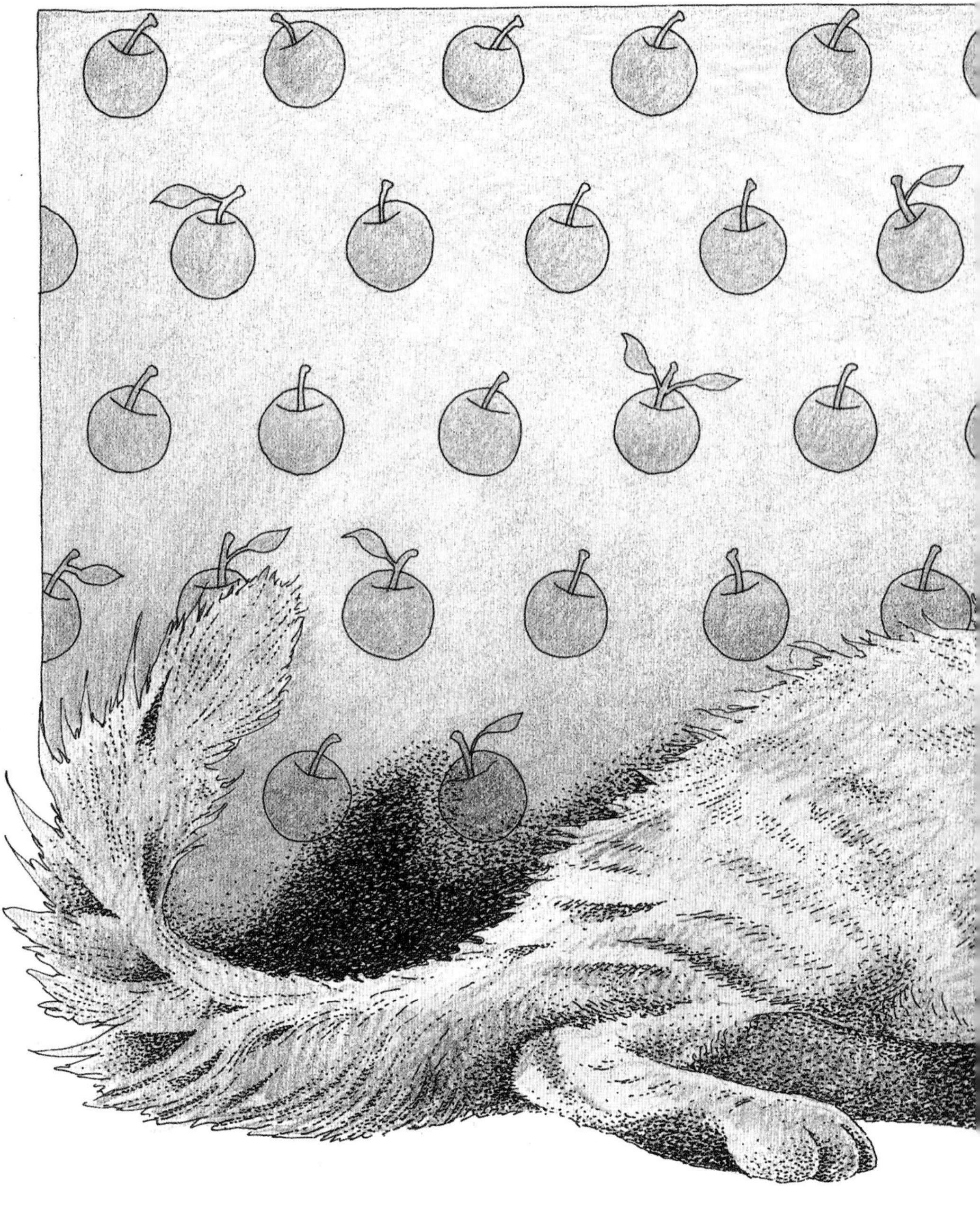

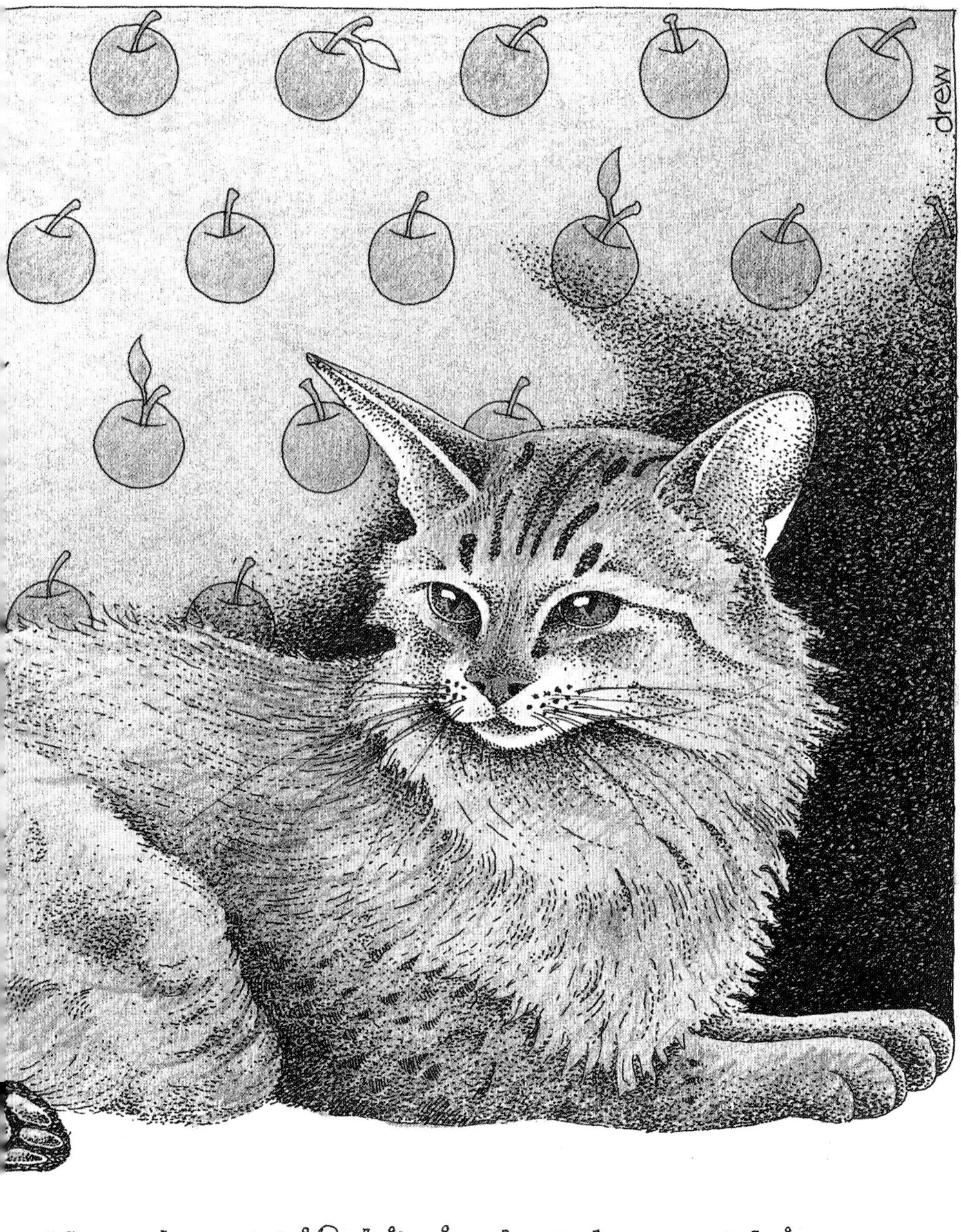
drew

How beautiful it is to do nothing
and then to rest afterwards.
spanish proverb

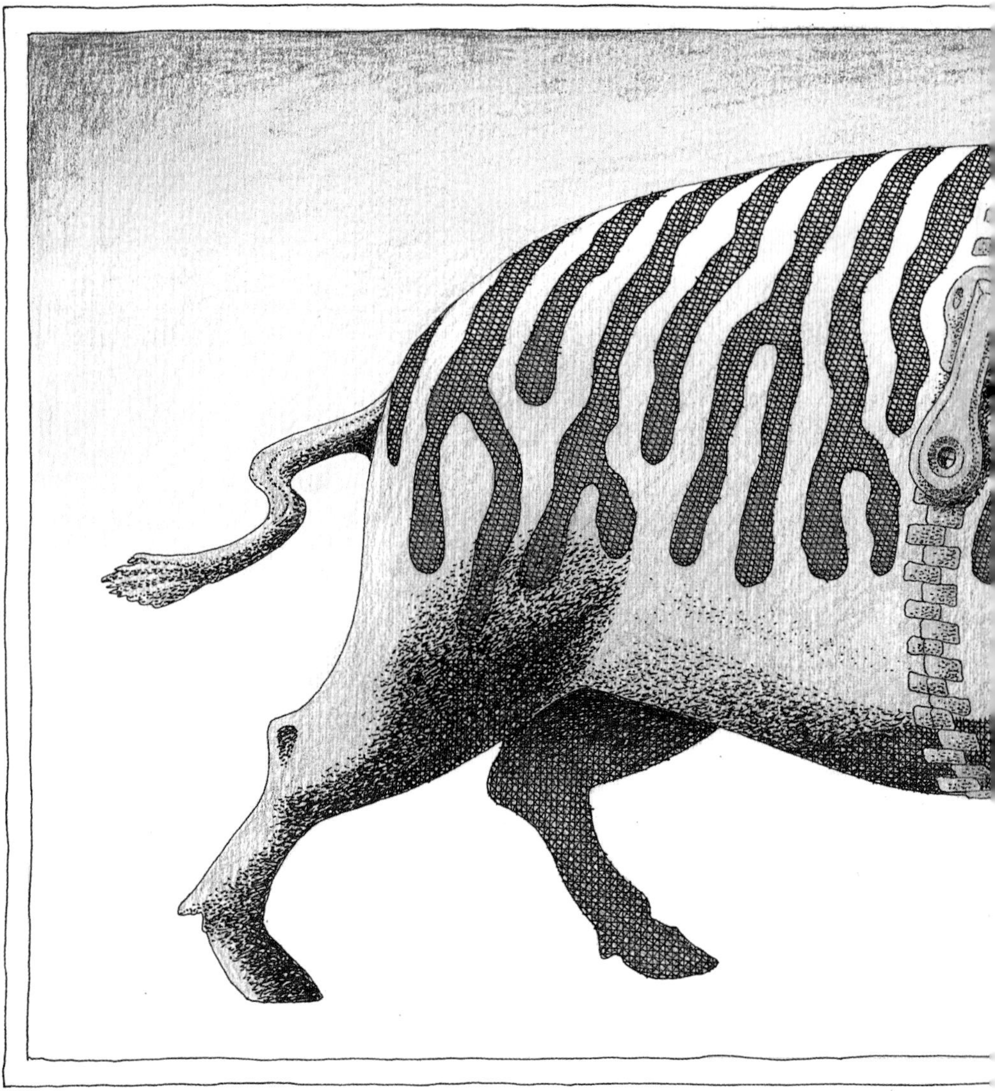

The Mysterious Disappearance of the Zepig

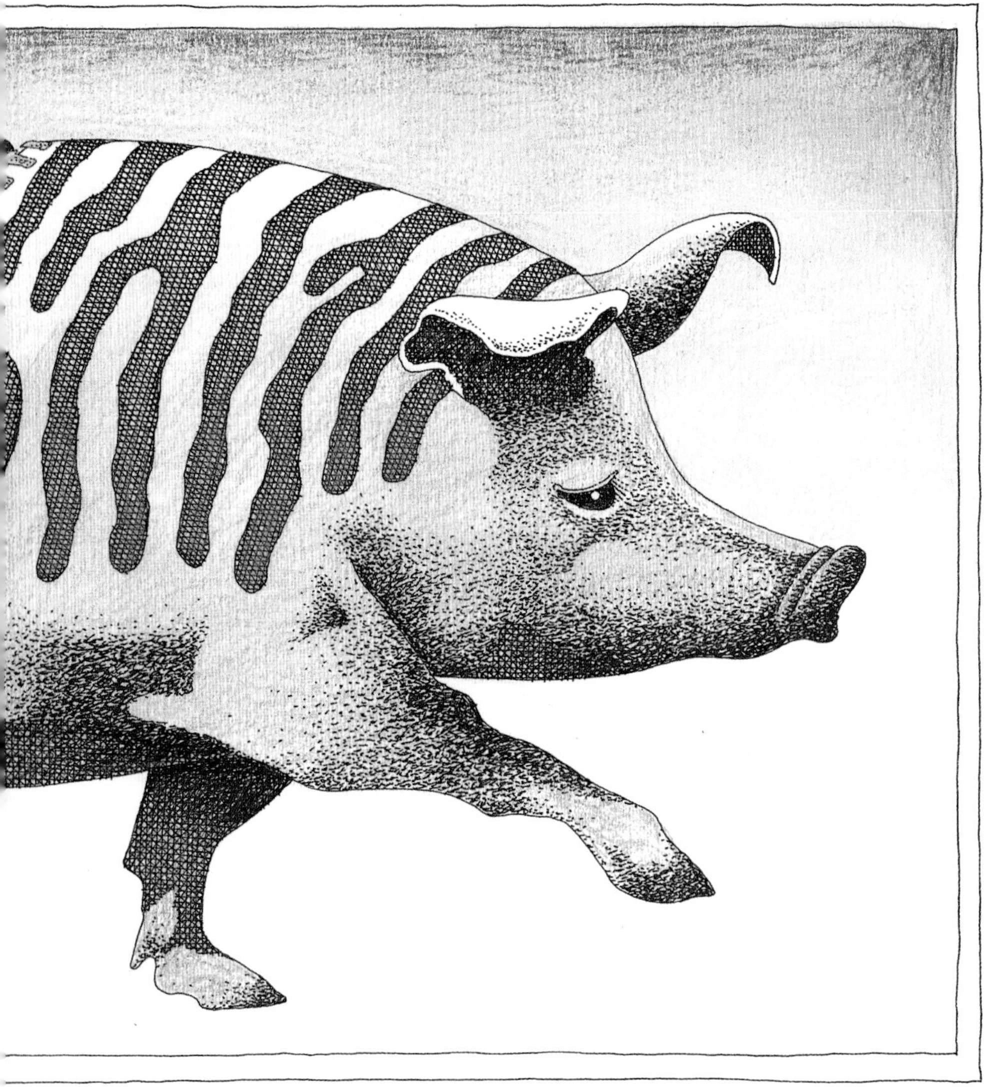

The zepig male while seeking love
had found a sow, and winked.
Despite his lust
she showed disgust.
(And now they're both extinct).

A Simple Guide to:
MOUNTAIN RECOGNITION

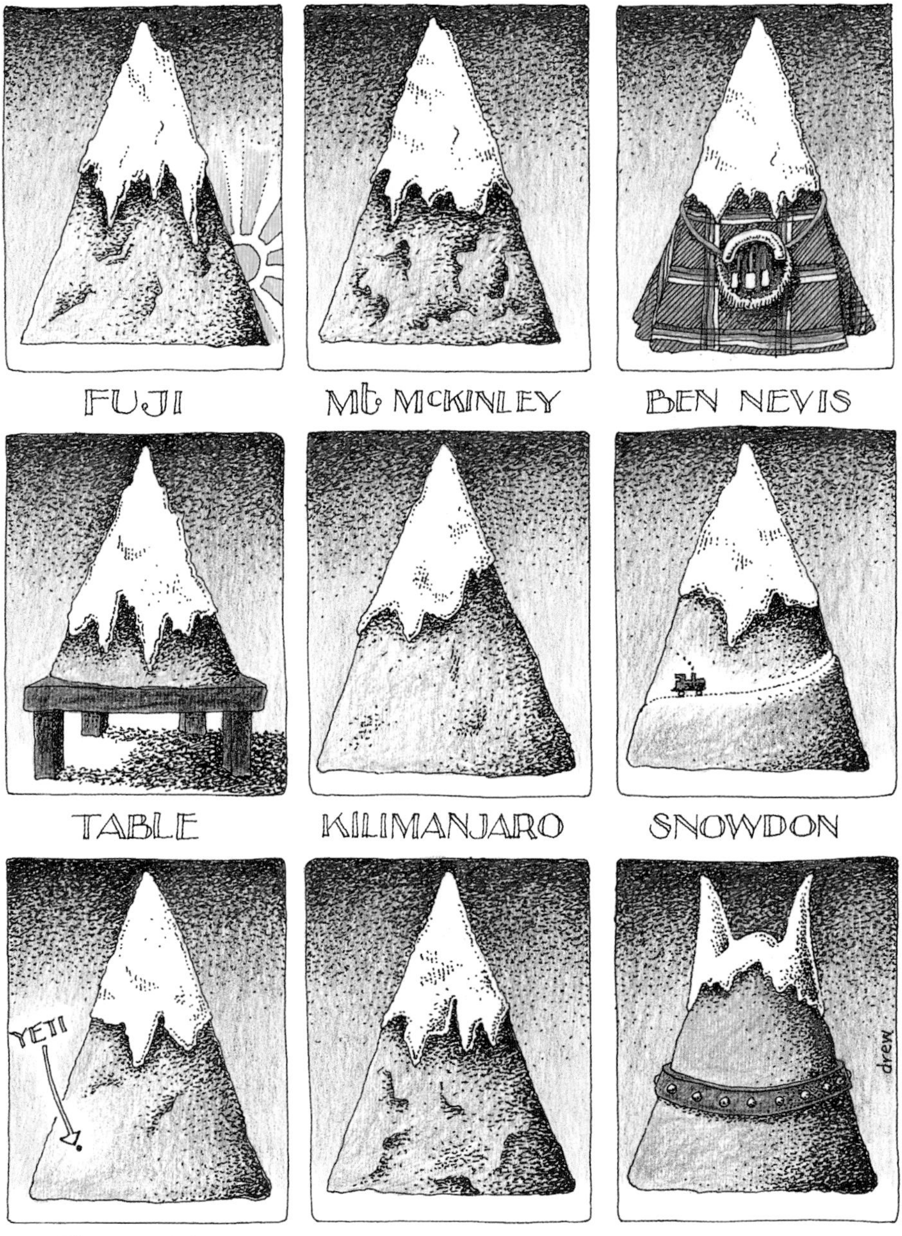
FUJI
Mt McKINLEY
BEN NEVIS
TABLE
KILIMANJARO
SNOWDON
YETI
EVEREST
K2
drew
K9

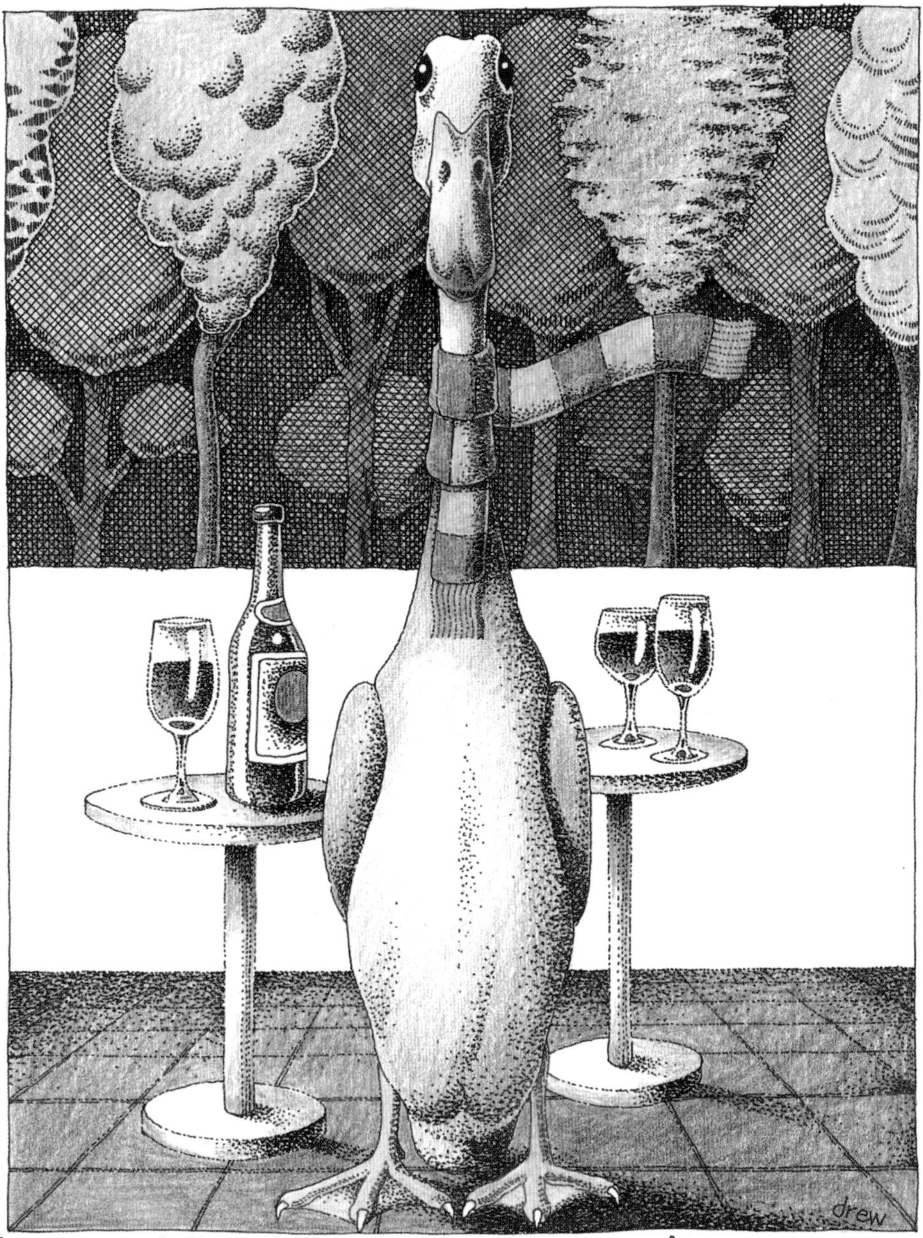
drew

'my problem is how to reconcile my net income with my gross habits' errol Flynn

SPOT THE ABBA SONG

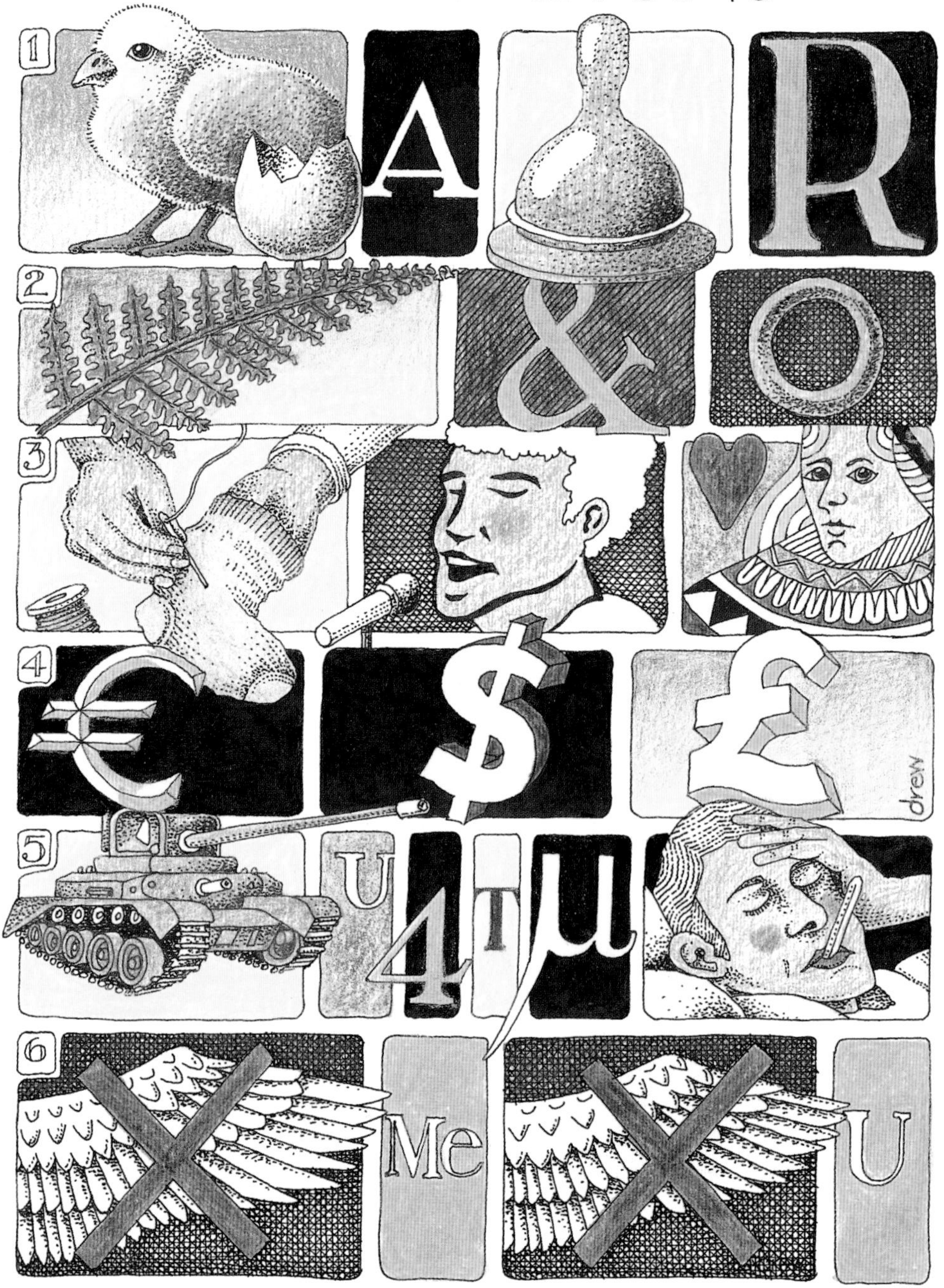

1
A
R
2
&
O
3
4
€
$
£
drew
5
U
4
T
μ
6
Me
U

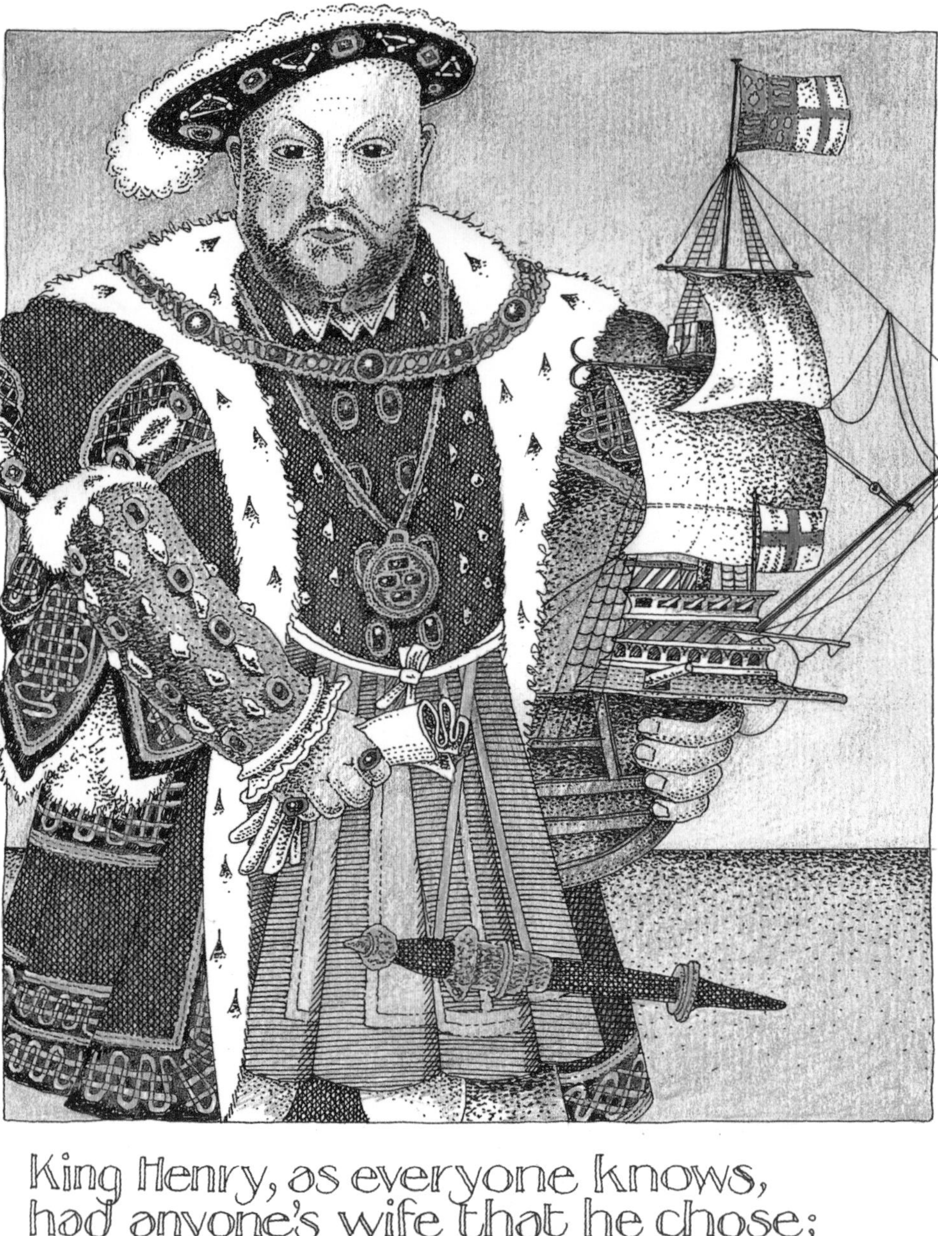

King Henry, as everyone knows,
had anyone's wife that he chose;
but very few knew
he'd a seventh wife too
and he gave her the name Mary Rose.